OLD MONEY

a play by

Wendy Wasserstein

SAMUEL FRENCH, INC.
45 WEST 25TH STREET   **NEW YORK 10010**
7623 SUNSET BOULEVARD   **HOLLYWOOD 90046**
LONDON   *TORONTO*

ISBN 0 573 62793 2   Printed in U.S.A.   #17709

IMPORTANT BILLING AND CREDIT REQUIREMENTS

LINCOLN CENTER THEATER
AT THE MITZI E. NEWHOUSE

under the direction of
André Bishop and Bernard Gersten

presents

OLD MONEY

a new play by
Wendy Wasserstein

with (in alphabetical order)

Emily Bergl	Charlie Hofheimer
Dan Butler	Mary Beth Hurt
John Cullum	Jodi Long
Mark Harelik	Kathryn Meisle

sets Thomas Lynch   costumes Jane Greenwood   lighting Mark McCullough

original music Lewis Flinn   sound Janet Kalas

choreography by John Carrafa

stage manager James FitzSimmons   casting Daniel Swee

director of development Hattie K. Jutagir   director of marketing/special projects Thomas Cott

general manager Steven C. Callahan   production manager Jeff Hamlin

directed by
Mark Brokaw

CAST OF CHARACTERS

(in order of appearance)

Ovid Walpole Bernstein/Tobias Pfeiffer II	CHARLIE HOFHEIMER
Jeffrey Bernstein/Arnold Strauss	MARK HARELIK
Flinty McGee/Florence DeRoot	KATHRYN MEISLE
Tobias Vivian Pfeiffer III/Schuyler Lynch	JOHN CULLUM
Sid Nercessian/Tobias Pfeiffer	DAN BUTLER
Penny Nercessian/Betina Brevoort	JODI LONG
Mary Gallagher/Caroline Nercessian	EMILY BERGL
Saulina Webb/Sally Webster	MARY BETH HURT

TIME and PLACE

A party on a Saturday night in August
in the private house of Jeffrey Bernstein
on Manhattan's Upper East Side.

The present.

For Ben Churchhill Wasserstein

ACT I

(A sunroom leading into the garden of a nineteenth-century Upper East Side mansion. The room, though impeccably restored, has a light and airy, almost gauze-like quality through which time and fashion can move easily. There is a banister leading to the upstairs. OVID WALPOLE BERNSTEIN, a seventeen-year-old boy, in standard chinos and blue shirt, steps forward. The present.)

OVID. My name is Ovid Walpole Bernstein and this is my house. Actually, it's my father's house. At the turn of the century it was the Manhattan mansion of Tobias Vivian Pfeiffer, who invented coal mining in West Virginia and the Tennessee and Topeka railroad. That's a little overstated but you get my drift.

The house was built by Schuyler Lynch of the architectural firm of Lynch, Oakes, and McTief, leading practitioners of the American Beaux Arts Movement. My house is the only remaining Lynch building in Manhattan currently in use as a private dwelling. The former Van Dressen mansion around the corner had a brief life in the 1930's as the Rex Club, an all-male dog-walking society, and as a Vidal Sassoon hair salon in the mid-sixties. It is currently before the zoning commission as a scientology center and singles hospitality cyber café. So we're in good company.

My parents bought this house in 1998, one year after my father's bank went public. Well, it's not really my father's bank, it doesn't have our name, but my father pioneered its fixed-income arbitrage into the largest trading desk in the world. At least that's the story according to the *Wall Street Journal*. When the bank went public, my father suddenly became an expert on Beaux Arts painting, Gulfstream jets, and Victorian lacquer lamps and furniture. Shortly after that time my mother and father's marriage broke up, as did the marriages of five of his managing partners.

My dad says you can divide the world into three groups: the players, those who wish they were players, and those who have absolutely no idea who the players are. He says life would be intolerable only in the middle category. My dad also says the lesson of Tobias Pfeiffer is you become a player by making up your own rules.

(JEFFREY BERNSTEIN, an attractive man of forty-eight in a very chic but defiantly casual linen suit, comes on stage. He has been listening to the later part of OVID's speech.)

JEFFREY. I never said that! What are you doing? I thought you were greeting our guests.

OVID. I'm preparing an introductory lecture for your party.

JEFFREY. This really isn't the ideal time or place for lectures.

OVID. But you seriously think the middle of August, when half the city is away, is the ideal time and place for a party?

JEFFREY. Ovey, if we had this party again in the Hamptons or Connecticut no one would have to make much of an effort to get here. Besides, hopefully this will take care of our social obligations for the next twenty years.

OVID. Well I invited someone because none of my friends are around. It's Tobias Pfeiffer's grandson.

JEFFREY. Pfeiffer's grandson has to be at least seventy!

OVID. No, better. Seventy-five. Tobias Vivian Pfeiffer III. He says his name is Vivian on his phone machine.

JEFFREY. How do you know him?

OVID. I don't. I read a review of his novel in the *Times*. So I called him. He taught the history of New York City at Columbia for fifty years. I love old maps and New York history stuff.

JEFFREY. Ovid, don't become the kind of dilettante intellectual who wastes his life dwelling on the past. It's great that you read, but read for a purpose. How's my suit?

OVID. It's nice. You've got that perfect "I'm just a regular guy who paid five thousand bucks for this shirt" look.

JEFFREY. I thought it was very casual.

OVID. Dad, when you were a boy did you think you'd be throwing parties in a robber baron's mansion?

JEFFREY. Not in August.

OVID. You haven't answered my question.

JEFFREY. You want to know if in my bunk bed on Coney Island Avenue I dreamed about becoming a hedge-fund analyst and not Davy Crockett?

OVID. Like, did all of your dreams come true?

JEFFREY. Don't say "like" Ovid. You're not from a suburban mall. *(He touches OVID's head.)* I'd say the dream that most came true for me was having you.

OVID. Dad, that's, like, really sentimental.

JEFFREY. OK, the most significant thing in my life was having you.

OVID. And money?

JEFFREY. Money what?

OVID. How important is money?

JEFFREY. In your case I'd say it's completely irrelevant.

OVID. And in your case?

JEFFREY. Money is the road to liberation, Ovid. Just ask any revolutionary.

(FLINTY McGEE, a well-groomed woman of thirty-five, simultaneously exuding professionalism and sexuality, comes into the room.)

FLINTY. Hi. I'm Flinty McGee.

OVID. The party impresario?

FLINTY. It's the kind of name you can't make up.

JEFFREY. I'm Jeffrey Bernstein. This is my son.

OVID. *(Shakes her hand.)* Ovid Walpole Bernstein. That's also the kind of name you can't make up. Are you getting my dad's party into Page Six of the *Chronicle*?

FLINTY. Oh, I'm not here in a professional capacity. Sid Nercessian's office invited me.

OVID. The film producer. Dad, Sid Nercessian is a friend of yours?

JEFFREY. He must be. He's inviting people to my party.

FLINTY. Well, I'm really friends with his wife Penny. She's such a brilliant businesswoman. She's my mentor, and I'm her social consultant.

OVID. Dad, why don't you have a social consultant?

FLINTY. Penny knew I've been dying to see this house. I loved the write-up in the Home Section. Penny says you did a spectacular restoration. She has such exquisite taste. I hope it's all right she invited me.

JEFFREY. Glad you could make it.

OVID. Me too.

FLINTY. It's very eccentric having your party in the city on a Saturday night in August. Although I must say that glorious front room is filling up.

OVID. We like the timing. Makes people really work to get here.

FLINTY. I'd love for you to tell me the history of this house.

OVID. Tobias Pfeiffer was born in Uniondale, Pennsylvania, in 1874.

JEFFREY. Not now, Ovid.

OVID. I thought ….

JEFFREY. You thought you were greeting our guests.

OVID. Would you excuse me, Miss McGee? I have to find a friend of mine.

(OVID exits.)

FLINTY. I always wanted to write a movie that takes place in this house. I pass it all the time. My shrink is around the corner.

JEFFREY. Are you a screenwriter as well as a publicist?

FLINTY. You can't seriously think I want to spend my entire life spinning the right buzz for parties and blow jobs.

JEFFREY. Does Sid Nercessian know about your film? Maybe he'll produce it.

FLINTY. The question is, why isn't Sid on his yacht somewhere in the Aegean?

JEFFREY. Miss McGee, maybe all our lives aren't what you crack them up to be.

FLINTY. Yours certainly is. You really interest me. Rhodes scholar, you started the *Yale Human Rights Law Journal*, worked as a teacher in a Head Start program in Tuscaloosa for two years. And now you're living in a house the *Times* called "the perfect evocation of a new gilded age."

JEFFREY. Do you think the kids I taught in Tuscaloosa would be better off if I didn't live here? I'll take you to my new best friend Sid.

FLINTY. I think I know exactly why Sid is showing up here tonight. He reveres real money. He's desperate to be put on that museum board, and you control it. He would sell his mother to be considered legit. Or he'd even offer you to produce a picture with him. Is that right?

JEFFREY. You're the expert on society, Miss McGee. I'm just a small businessman.

(VIVIAN PFEIFFER, a man in his mid-seventies in a rumpled-from-the-heat seersucker suit, enters. Once obviously quite handsome, he appears faded yet courtly.)

VIVIAN. Is this the smoking room?

JEFFREY. I'd prefer you didn't.

VIVIAN. Are you our host?

JEFFREY. Yes.

VIVIAN. Vivian Pfeiffer. Your son invited me. I just met him in the front room. Fascinating young man. Wonderful sense of the past.

JEFFREY. We're delighted you could make it.

VIVIAN. I certainly had no other invitations tonight, and my air-conditioning is broken.

JEFFREY. And this is Flinty McGee.

VIVIAN. Of course. The "holy arbiter of the new A-list."

FLINTY. Please. I'm just another PR girl.

VIVIAN. Not according to the *New York Chronicle*.

FLINTY. That was a total puff piece.

VIVIAN. I wouldn't have minded a puff piece instead of the autopsy they just performed on my book.

FLINTY. Are you a writer?

VIVIAN. Only obscure novels that sell when the good ladies of

Rochester realize there isn't a Louis Auchincloss left they haven't already read.

JEFFREY. Mr. Pfeiffer taught New York City History at Columbia for fifty years.

VIVIAN. Yes, I'm practically the last living dead white man.

FLINTY. Did you grow up in this house?

VIVIAN. Lived here till I was twelve. My father Tobey was raised here and married my mother in this garden. I must compliment you on your restoration, Mr. Bernstein. What I've seen so far is exact.

FLINTY. Mr. Pfeiffer, I'd love to do you for the *Chronicle*.

VIVIAN. "Do me?"

FLINTY. Every now and then I do a little profile at the *Chronicle*. They let me cause I throw all their parties. Old and new money are kind of my obsession. The Trumps, the Koches, the Miller sisters, I love all that. You see, Mr. Pfeiffer, in your day it was all about bloodlines. Over fifty percent of the richest men in American were also on the social register. But now society has merged with celebrity. Cash frankly has superseded class. We live in an asset-based meritocracy. There are sixty-four new millionaires a day in Silicon Valley, and no one cares where they come from. So everything's much more democratic.

VIVIAN. God bless America. You're not from New York, are you, Miss McGee?

FLINTY. No.

VIVIAN. I'd guess a small mid western town.

FLINTY. Independence, Kansas. Not that small. Why?

VIVIAN. Only someone who wasn't from this world would become so enamoured of it. You need to take it more for granted. Then you'll never give yourself away.

FLINTY. Thank you. Jeffrey, would you show me the garden?

VIVIAN. Miss McGee, you'll be interested to know that the garden is the only one in Manhattan that Schuyler Lynch, the architect of this house, designed himself. The garden incorporated Lynch's theories of the lush picturesque as opposed to the minimal nature of most Upper East Side gardens. The gazebo, by the way, was suggested by a Miss Florence DeRoot, a well-known decorator, who for many years was my grandfather's mistress.

JEFFREY. That's very helpful, Mr. Pfeiffer.

VIVIAN. Forgive me for lecturing. It's an occupational hazard. I haven't been in front of a classroom for a year, so I seize every opportunity I get.

JEFFREY. Help yourself. My son and I are fascinated by new York City history.

FLINTY. Oh, me too. I love it!

(JEFFREY opens the door leading to the garden. VIVIAN sits down and picks up a violin from the chair.)

VIVIAN. Whose violin?

JEFFREY. That's Ovid's. He was planning to join in with some friends who are coming tonight from the Philharmonic.

FLINTY. We used a garden quartet for the colitis lunch at the Frick. There's nothing I love more than a summer quartet in a garden gazebo.

JEFFREY and FLINTY exit. VIVIAN takes a glass of water from a tray as SID and PENNY enter. They are both around forty. He wears a T-shirt, jacket and sneakers. PENNY is a beautiful Asian woman who is assuredly elegant-looking.)

SID. Fuck me. Or is this some beautiful house!

PENNY. Sid, I wonder if these were the original ceilings, or did they have them put in?

VIVIAN. They were the original ceilings. Prime examples of Schuyler Lynch's eccentricity and modern sense of whimsical ornamentation.

SID. Who are you? We were told our host was here.

VIVIAN. He's in the garden with Miss McGee.

PENNY. Flinty was dying to see this garden. Asa Kent did it. He just did Vera's in Southampton. He's so minimal but real.

SID. Fuck minimal! Give me trees.

PENNY. Honey, if you don't like what Asa did here, we can go with someone else for our house. But he's first on everyone's list.

SID. You're the one with perfect taste. What's that?

VIVIAN. Water.
PENNY. What kind of water?
VIVIAN. I believe it's Evian.
PENNY. From a glass or plastic bottle?
SID. It's water. You just fucking drink it.
PENNY. Sid, I can taste the difference. I promised Bob we'd commit to purity in all aspects of our life.
SID. Who the hell is Bob?
PENNY. Our feng shui master.
SID. That crook! He used to work at the Door Store.
PENNY. You asked me to help you balance your life.
SID. We'll find Bernstein and ask him.

(SID and PENNY exit into the garden. MARY GALLAGHER, a gamine waitress in a formal uniform, comes in the room.)

VIVIAN. Miss, could you tell me if this is from a glass or plastic bottle?
MARY. Beg your pardon, sir?
VIVIAN. Never mind. *(He sits down.)*

(The band starts to play "Ta Ra Ra Boom De Ay" and a handsome man of seventeen dressed in a school uniform from around 1917 comes into the room carrying a bag. The young man is TOBIAS PFEIFFER II, known as Tobey. He is played by the same actor who plays OVID. He mimes carrying a rifle and makes shooting noises.)

TOBEY. Alleyman. Alleyman. Take cover! Take cover!
MARY. Mr. Pfeiffer!
TOBEY. Miss Gallagher!
VIVIAN. Father!
MARY. What are you doing home?
TOBEY. There's no reason to be in New Hampshire in August when I can be with a beautiful girl in New York. *(He lifts her up.)*
MARY. Shouldn't you be at school?
TOBEY. Shouldn't you be in the kitchen?

MARY. Your father is having people to supper tonight.

TOBEY. In August? Shouldn't they be up in Newport?

MARY. Your father says the war changes everything. Mr. Pfeiffer?

TOBEY. Miss Gallagher?

MARY. Who was Archduke Ferdinand and why should we care?

TOBEY. You're not worried about the collapse of the Ottoman Empire, Miss Gallagher?

MARY. Not really. Should I tell your father you're here?

VIVIAN. No. It's a surprise for him.

TOBEY. No. It's a surprise for him. *(He takes a flask from his jacket.)* Miss Gallagher, can I interest you in an aperitif?

MARY. Oh no. I should be giving a final check on the library. You know how your father likes to smoke with the men after supper.

TOBEY. Bores me silly. That's why I want to go into show business.

MARY. Really!

VIVIAN. Really!

MARY. Show business. I'll have a drink. *(Pours a bit from the flask.)*

VIVIAN. I'll have a drink *(Pours a bit from the flask.)*

TOBEY. I was head of the Dramatic Club at St. Paul's School, you know. I'd like to direct musical shows and maybe even write them too.

MARY. Your father won't let you write musical shows. You'll be going to Princeton and then directly into his business. You'll be taking over this house one day.

TOBEY. I have a Jewish friend at school who says his father will give us the money to do our shows.

MARY. I thought all the Jews lived on the Lower East Side.

TOBEY. He started a movie studio in California. His mother is a silent-film star. You'd like him a lot. He's in my summer training regiment.

MARY. Your father is having Mr. Arnold Strauss, the department store owner, to dinner tonight. He doesn't seem Jewish at all. Florence DeRoot says Mr. Strauss is using your father to get on the museum board. She says she can spot a climber a mile away. But I say, takes one to know one. I never said that.

VIVIAN. Lips are sealed.

(TOBEY picks up the violin.)

TOBEY. Is there going to be music tonight?

MARY. A chamber group from the Philharmonic.

TOBEY. The Philharmonic? But my father doesn't even like classical music.

MARY. Miss DeRoot says she's teaching your father how to live like old money.

TOBEY. Who cares about all that? Do you know why I want to go into show business, Mary? Because no one cares what your real name is. I can say I'm Tobey Viviano and grew up on Mott Street. *(Picks up the violin.)* My papa came to his country from Parma in 1903. *(Hits a chord.)* He had a parmigiana cheese cart and wrote a song each time he sold a piece. *(Hits another chord.)* Then one dark night there was a knock on the door. It was the police with a papal decree. *(Hits another chord.)* "Viviano, you are a nuisance with your cheese and silly songs. You must leave this country tonight." My father said, "Don't worry, Mama. We will go to America where I can write songs on Tin Pan Alley, the Ziegfeld girls will dance and George M. Cohan will sing!" *(Hits another chord and sings:)*

Ta ra ra boom de ay

Ta ra ra boom de ay

(MARY GALLAGHER sings along. TOBEY and MARY begin dancing together. VIVIAN sings along and makes kazoo noises. They continue to dance off into the kitchen. VIVIAN sings and claps. JEFFREY and FLINTY come back into the room and watch VIVIAN singing in the empty room.)

JEFFREY. Mr. Pfeiffer, I'm so glad you're enjoying the music. They do a very nice turn-of-the-century suite.

VIVIAN. *(Catching himself.)* Yes. Yes, it's very authentic.

(SID and PENNY reenter.)

SID. Jeffrey, this is some party! It's fucking August fourth in Manhattan, and you've got Henry Kravis and Charlie Rose schvitzing in the garden.

FLINTY. Makes total sense to me. I hate Martha's Vineyard in the summer now. If I have to see one more orthodontist's wife carrying a straw whaling purse, I'm just going to scream. And the Hamptons aren't even worth discussing. At least where you are in Nantucket is still livable.

SID. There's no fucking food! Every meal is corn and lobster buried in sand! Whey do they do that? These people are not fucking whalers! They're Jews!

JEFFREY. Didn't you just buy the two adjoining properties?

PENNY. Sid's just being Sid. We're just waiting for the town board approval before we start.

JEFFREY. How many rooms will it be?

PENNY. Around thirty-six. Our plan is to go modern and light.

VIVIAN. My family used to visit the Wylies every summer in Nantucket. I always thought the joy of that island was the architectural uniformity. Not even the sea captains' houses had more than twelve rooms.

PENNY. Mr. Pfeiffer, we're very committed to preserving the architectural integrity of the island.

VIVIAN. I never like it. Too white, too Republican.

SID. *(Puts his arm around his wife.)* We'll fix that.

VIVIAN. Yes. Well, that's progress. Would you excuse me? *(Exits.)*

SID. Who the hell is that?

JEFFREY. Writer. Grew up in this house.

SID. Wait a minute. That guy grew up in this house? This is beyond depressing! Fuck! If you told me Jeffrey Katzenberg grew up in this house, that would make sense to me.

FLINTY. I don't think Jews lived in these houses.

SID. Thank you, Henry James. Honey, was it Henry James who wrote that Scorsese movie with Winona?

PENNY. *Age of Innocence.* That's an Edith Wharton movie.

SID. Well, thank you, Edith Wharton. How much would you say Katzenberg is worth?

FLINTY. I'd say five hundred.

SID. No, no way. I'd say under four. Katzenberg's not real money. He couldn't afford this house. Don't you think so, Jeffrey?

FLINTY. I bet Bernstein's mother taught him never to talk about money in public.

PENNY. What's your point, Sid?

SID. My point is Katzenberg still has to work for a living. Even with the Disney settlement. He doesn't have enough fuck-you money to stop. Katzenberg's poor. Bill Gates, even when they split him in half, makes a decent living.

JEFFREY. But you never know. Katzenberg is still young.

SID. Gwyneth is young! Those boys in their underwear on the cover of *Vanity Fair* are young.

FLINTY. Did you see that cover, Jeffrey? It was all Penny's underwear.

SID. It's her new "Bite Me" line. I gave her the name. Compared to those cover boys Katzenberg isn't even middle-aged. He's an alta kaka just like us.

JEFFREY. What's that?

SID. You're bull shitting me.

PENNY. Jeffrey, it's an old cocker. Sid's been teaching me. We're celebrating my conversion next week. We'd love if you and Flinty would come. Sid, I think it's time to feed the baby.

JEFFREY. Did you bring her with you? I'd love to see her.

PENNY. Bethesda's home with the nanny and the night nurse. We do Breast Express.

FLINTY. Oh, I heard about that. Sounds fantastic!

SID. It's the best fucking thing since Mallomars. We can go anywhere. Penny pumps the milk and the Wells Fargo wagon is right there waiting. Baby doesn't even know the fucking difference.

PENNY. I swear those guys have saved my life. It's the only way I've been able to work and still cope.

SID. Breast Express driver plus trainer and nurse technician is a fucking bargain at five thousand a week! Flinty, give yourself a treat and watch my wife feed our children. It'll make a nice little item for the *Chronicle*.

FLINTY. Sid, find me a man just like you.

(PENNY and FLINTY exit.)

SID. You could have her upstairs in half an hour.

JEFFREY. I'm having a party.

SID. Jeffrey, thank God you're better with money than you are with women. I'm not talking about love, Jeffrey. Just goddamn sex.

(OVID walks in the room.)

OVID. What are you talking about?

SID. Movies. Did you know your father's going into the movies?

OVID. Dad, you didn't tell me this.

SID. What's the point of being rich, Ovid, unless it gives you the ability to play? Your dad's going to be one of the producers of my next film. Best lesson in life he can teach you is there's nothing more satisfying that doing good work.

JEFFREY. What do you think of this idea, Ovey? Sid wants to update Sheridan's *The Rivals.*

OVID. The eighteenth-century post-Restoration comedy?

SID. Smart kid.

OVID. We read it in tenth grade.

JEFFREY. Great idea, don't you think?

SID. Well, Kenny Branagh wants to do it. And we'll put in Buffy the Vampire Slayer as Lydia Whatshername, and it'll be cutting and edgy and I think have something to really say about all our fucked-up values today. A sort of *American Beauty* meets *Shakespeare in Love* with a touch of *Sense and Sensitivity.*

OVID. Just one more thing. Buffy the Vampire Slayer is over.

SID. Where did you hear that?

OVID. Everyone at Trinity says that.

SID. My kid goes to Dalton. How come she never told me this? I'm gonna fucking kill her. *(He calls into the hall.)* Caroline! Caroline! Where the fuck are you?

(CAROLINE, a gamine, very hip teenager, walks into the room. She is played by the same actor who plays MARY.)

SID. Why didn't you tell me Buffy the Vampire is over?

CAROLINE. How should I know where your specific interests lie?

SID. Is that how your mother teaches you to speak to me?

CAROLINE. My mother says I shouldn't speak to you at all. I only came to see this house. Oh and Dad, I have a message for you from your wife. Something's wrong with the Breast Express van. The police won't let them park in front of the house.

JEFFREY. What?

SID. Bernstein, what the fuck is going on here? A child's life is at stake!

(He runs out of the room. JEFFREY follows him.)

CAROLINE. Can you believe this place?

OVID. Sort of. I'm Ovid Bernstein. I live here.

CAROLINE. Isn't it, like, embarrassing? This house is off the hook. It's so not downtown.

OVID. I don't go downtown much.

CAROLINE. What do you do? Your homework?

OVID. My dad wants me to go to Princeton.

CAROLINE. What do you want?

OVID. Me? I don't know. Maybe I'll be a writer. I have an idea for a novel.

CAROLINE. I'm not going to college.

OVID. You're not?

CAROLINE. No. I got into Brown, but I'm going to L.A. I'm going to get a job as a topless dancer.

OVID. You mean you're taking a year off for life experience.

CAROLINE. Yeah, sort of. Well, I want to never be really frightened. My mother, is, like terrified of everything. Since my dad left mother has had her eyes, her nose, and her throat done. My mother has thirty million from her divorce and no confidence at all.

OVID. Does she work?

CAROLINE. Well, she has a lot of work done. Sometimes I kind of think it makes much more sense to end it all now instead of wasting more of my time and parents' money. Like, last year I tried to kill myself three times, once with pills, once with Draino, and the last time with a Swiss Army knife.

OVID. That's terrible! What about your mother?

CAROLINE. My mother would have more time for her masseuses and her yoga trainer.

OVID. Well, I would miss you.

CAROLINE. That's a totally whack thing to say. You don't even know me.

OVID. My mother always said when I paid attention, I was very good about people.

CAROLINE. Is she?

OVID. She died last year. They were separated and the divorce hadn't exactly come through yet. This is our first party since then. She was a musician. She taught me to play the violin. My father says you have to play music for a purpose.

CAROLINE. To get into Princeton?

OVID. Something like that.

CAROLINE. Oh screw him! Wanna see something?

OVID. Sure.

CAROLINE. *(Begins to roll up her dress to show him a tattoo on her pelvis.)* I got this tattoo when my dad made that update of *Citizen Kane* with Matt Damon. It's a rosebud.

OVID. Like the sled. Cool.

CAROLINE. Wanna touch it?

OVID. Well, maybe not here. I mean, a guest could walk in, or your father.

CAROLINE. Oh, he's seen me do this before. But I understand if you wanna see it upstairs in your room.

OVID. My father kinda counts on me to cohost with him.

CAROLINE. You're cohosting me. I'm dying to take a tour of this house. We studied it in Advanced Placement History.

OVID. You're into history?

CAROLINE. "Seeds of Revolution: From Robber Barons to Emma Goldman." That was the title of my senior paper.

OVID. C'mon. I'll give you the deluxe upstairs tour. *(Takes her hand.)* But don't put your hands on the banister. We have it polished twice a day.

CAROLINE. I wish you hadn't told me that.

(She leans her entire body on the banister as they go upstairs. OVID leans his body on the banister too. They giggle as they go upstairs. VIVIAN walks into the room and notices them.)

VIVIAN. Mr. Bernstein! You'll be glad to know that life has improved since I lived here. My father would never let me touch the banister unless I had gloves on.

OVID. Mr. Pfeiffer, would you excuse us? I have to help Caroline with her homework.

VIVIAN. In the middle of August?

OVID. We're performing a play.

CAROLINE. *The Rivals.*

OVID. She's Lydia Whatshername.

(They both burst out giggling and run upstairs. The quartet begins playing one of the "Brandenburg Concertos." VIVIAN picks up the violin and beings to play along. TOBIAS PFEIFFER, played by the same actor who plays SID NERCESSIAN, and FLORENCE DeROOT, played by the same actor who plays FLINTY, enter the room. PFEIFFER and FLORENCE are dressed in white formal summer clothes. FLORENCE is overdone but quite glamorous. PFEIFFER looks hot and bothered by the suit.)

PFEIFFER. Jesus, it's hot. Why do I have to sit around in August in my own house with a bunch of old biddies eating lobster thermidor?

FLORENCE. Betina Brevoort and Sally Webster are from two of the best New York families.

PFEIFFER. They're still old biddies.

FLORENCE. Tobias, remember you're the head of the museum nominating committee. We worked very had to get you that.

PFEIFFER. Did you choose this music?

VIVIAN. Grandfather, it's a "Brandenburg Concerto."

PFEIFFER. Sounds German. Is this the crap you told me Carnegie likes?

FLORENCE. It's Bach, dear.

PFEIFFER. Why don't they play, "It's a Long Way to Tippe-rary"?

FLORENCE. Tobias, if we build a Pfeiffer concert hall in your honor, you should learn to enjoy classical music.

PFEIFFER. I like the opera. Big girls with elephants. Isn't that enough?

VIVIAN. Fine. All right with you, Miss DeRoot?

FLORENCE. Fine. We'll build an opera house. We can have a much better party for the opening of an opera house. Even Mrs. Astor would have to come.

PFEIFFER. Damn it. That music is getting on my nerves. Play "Tipperary"!

VIVIAN. Yes sir!

(VIVIAN begins to play "It's a Long Way to Tipperary" along with the other musicians as TOBEY and MARY dance out of the kitchen. TOBEY sings:)

TOBEY.
That's the wrong way
To tickle Mary,
That's the wrong way
To kiss.

(TOBEY starts to kiss MARY.)

VIVIAN. Father!

MARY. *(Suddenly stops when she sees TOBIAS PFEIFFER and FLORENCE. Startled.)* Mr. Pfeiffer!

FLORENCE. Shouldn't you be attending to the guests Mary?

TOBEY. I'm a guest, Madame.

PFEIFFER. No you're not. You live here. What are you doing home?

TOBEY. I came down to see you Father.

PFEIFFER. Well, you've picked an inconvenient time. I'm hav-ing some important people here tonight. This is Miss Florence

DeRoot.

FLORENCE. I've heard so much about you, Tobey. *(To PFEIF-FER:)* Dear, I'll ask the musicians to try a little Vivaldi. *(To TOBEY:)* Your father loves Vivaldi. Especially *The Four Seasons*.

TOBEY. Which season do you like the most, Father?

PFEIFFER. The one they charge the least to play. Don't you think you should be getting dressed for dinner? Or would you prefer I tell my guests my son is an anarchist.

TOBEY. Yes, sir! *(Begins to run up the steps.)*

PFEIFFER. I told you never to touch the banister. Costs me at least two dollars a week to keep that polished.

FLORENCE. Mary, it's always so much more *au currant* to have the roses on the side table and the lilies in Mr. Pfeiffer's cut crystal vases. *Merci. (Takes PFEIFFER's arm.)* There is nothing I love for more than a summer quartet in a garden gazebo.

VIVIAN. Mary Gallagher, can you keep a secret? I'm very intimidated by my grandfather. And if it makes you feel any better, he never married Florence DeRoot.

MARY. Now that is a happy ending!

VIVIAN. After they parted, she was forced to join the working class as a full-time decorator.

MARY. You mean she was hanging curtains?

VIVIAN. She invented the window treatment.

MARY Jesus! Don't this story just be getting better and better!

VIVIAN. No one ever told you this?

MARY. I died of a splinter by then.

VIVIAN. A splinter?

MARY. Staph infection. Misdiagnosed tonight at Bellevue Hospital. There's something about surviving I just never learned.

VIVIAN. We have that in common, Mary Gallagher.

MARY. Really, if life were fair, I should have married your father. Been a rich lady myself.

VIVIAN. It might not have been very much fun.

MARY. Nonsense.

VIVIAN. My father became a frugal and devoutly religious man. He devoted the later part of his life to philanthropy. In every town that my grandfather busted a union, my father built Pfeiffer libraries and

Pfeiffer hospitals. He gave his entire fortune away.

MARY. None to you.

VIVIAN. No.

MARY. If he had married me, none of this would have happened.

VIVIAN. Mary Gallagher, I have a confession to make. Despite my medical conditions, I don't take any painkillers. But I made an exception tonight. I summoned up all my resources just to get here. I have questions only this house can answer.

MARY. Well, I can't be helping you. I should be getting to work before Mrs. DeRoot sees the vases in the front parlor.

VIVIAN. Miss Gallagher, may I trouble you for a favor? I remember the past so much more vividly than the present. Can you tell me if we are really having this conversation?

MARY. Of course we are. I don't spend my time just talking to the air. *(Exits.)*

VIVIAN. I don't mind losing my breath or my powers of digestion, but I will not lose my ability to reason. There should be a hidden passageway just behind this sculpture. As a child I used to hide there. It was the only place I felt safe. Do you mind if I move this object which seems to be in the way? It's far heavier than it needs to be.

(He begins moving a large sculpture. As he does, SAULINA WEBB, around forty-five, a downtown artist not chic in black, comes into the room. SAULINA does not keep herself well.)

SAULINA. That's mine.

VIVIAN. Excuse me.

SAULINA. I made that sculpture. I would appreciate your being careful with it.

VIVIAN. I was looking for a secret passage to the servants' quarters. This should lead to the side door.

SAULINA. You mean to a safe. What have you taken so far? The art here isn't really worth that much. Unless you're wild for American impressionism from the Marlborough Gallery.

VIVIAN. Actually, I'm a friend of Ovid's,

SAULINA. Are you in the same class at school?

VIVIAN. He invited me tonight after he read the review of one of my novels.

SAULINA. He should have at least read the book. I'm Ovey's Aunt Saulina. Was it a good review?

VIVIAN. No. It was rather unfavorable. "Tobias Vivian Pfeiffer, III, is not as talented a guide to the human heart has he is to the streets of New York." Who knows? Maybe they were right.

SAULINA. Are you Pfeiffer as in this house?

VIVIAN. Yes.

SAULINA. Then they were wrong. Men named Vivian who grew up in houses with secret passageways and still wear seersucker suits tend to be very sensitive souls. My studio art professors at RISD were all like you. Gay and aesthetically pure.

VIVIAN. I see you like to make generalizations about people as well as their art.

SAULINA. Sorry. You live in Greenwich with Muffy and the five kids and never regretted a day of it.

VIVIAN. Actually, I've lived most of my life alone. Over the years I've had a variety of unavailable crushes. But generally I far prefer waking up solo, early, and heading straight for my desk.

SAULINA. Yes. There's nothing more heavenly than breakfast for one.

(SID and FLINTY walk in with JEFFREY.)

JEFFREY. Saulina!

SAULINA.   Hello, Jeffrey. *(She immediately grabs VIVIAN's hand.)*

SAULINA. Ovid invited me.

VIVIAN. He's quite the host!

FLINTY. Saulina?

SAULINA. Named for my uncle Saul. He died at the track.

SID. Wait a minute! I know you! You're Saulina Webb. The sculptor. The Tampon Totem Pole. Oldenberg, but feminist.

SAULINA. Actually, I was experimenting with feminine textures: cotton, rubber, bobby pins.

SID. You don't have to explain to me. Jane Fonda collected you.

OLD MONEY

You're due for a comeback.

JEFFREY. This is one of Saulina's sculptures.

SID. I wouldn't have guessed.

SAULINA. It's from my normal period.

FLINTY. I just want you to know that I completely disagree with that recent *New Yorker* piece you were mentioned in.

SID. What *New Yorker* piece?

FLINTY. Some hack nobody reads said Saulina's type of feminist art was dated and retro.

SAULINA. It wasn't a hack. It was the dean of the Yale Art School.

SID. Academics. What the fuck do they know?

VIVIAN. Would you like to see my old room, Saulina. Third floor, last one on the left.

JEFFREY. That's Ovid's room.

SID. I'd like to see it. Jeffrey, we could shoot my update of *The Rivals* right here. Use all New York actors. Save at least ten million!

(VIVIAN, SAULINA, and SID exit.)

FLINTY. Did I do something wrong?

JEFFREY. No. I just haven't seen Saulina since my wife passed away.

FLINTY. Was that deliberate?

JEFFREY. Let's just say we both managed to make it happen.

FLINTY. Weren't you and Jessica separated when she died?

JEFFREY. Flinty, these are rhetorical questions, since you obviously know all the answers.

FLINTY. I hate dealing with someone so much smarter than me.

JEFFREY. No one told me how very ill Jessica was. She died at home with Saulina. They were watching Greer Garson in *Pride and Prejudice*. I was away with Ovid on a business trip in Prague, Saulina and I haven't spoken since.

FLINTY. She seems a little tightly wound.

JERRFRY. Saulina was my best friend in college. She introduced me to Jessica.

FLINTY. Well, they certainly were different!

JEFFREY. You knew Jessica?

FLINTY. I did the Chamber Music Spring Gala. She was the chair.

JEFFREY. She wasted too much time on those things. Makes much more sense just to send a check.

FLINTY. But Jessica enjoyed it.

JEFFREY. And you? Do you enjoy it? You're obviously gifted at it.

FLINTY. Bernstein, you've got to look at the bigger picture. Last spring I did the Costume Institute Gala. Now do I really care if Audrey Hepburn's entire Givenchy wardrobe is preserved? But everybody you ever read about was there. All of the "It" girls are swapping baby pictures while Puff Daddy is off whispering to Henry Kissinger. And of course Robert's flowers are to die for. I just feel so lucky to be right in the middle of it. I love my life. And you should too.

JEFFREY. Who says that I don't?

FLINTY. All I'm saying is, people with real money owe it to society to keep themselves and their children thoroughly enjoying it. Because if the rich aren't happy, then who the hell will be? You set the standard.

JEFFREY. So it's sort of a Thorsten Veblen trickle-down theory.

FLINTY. I don't know what it is, Bernstein. I didn't go to Yale. I went to North Central Kansas State.

JEFFREY. Did anyone ever tell you you've got the sweetest crinkle right there when you get angry. *(He touches her forehead.)*

FLINTY. I really shouldn't have that. That's where I just got my botox injection. I better call Dr. Waxman.

JEFFREY. I like it. Don't call Dr. Waxman.

FLINTY. Bernstein, let me be up-front with you.

JEFFREY. I wouldn't say you've been precisely holding back.

FLINTY. I'm here because I'm putting my dibs in early. For Christ's sake, you're already number fourteen on the *Chronicle's* list of New York's most eligible bachelors.

JEFFREY. Thirteen. And I already have a number of candidates. And there's a waiting list.

FLINTY. I don't intimidate you at all.

JEFFREY. Money insulates people. Flinty, you're our Boswell. You more than anyone should know that. *(Kisses her cheek. SAULINA comes back into the room.)* Tour over so soon?

SAULINA. I left my cigarettes. Vivian is telling Ovid and Sid stories about lost New York. He says life was much more fun then. There was always something to look forward to.

FLINTY. I'm sure with all the artists you know in New York, Saulina, you have something to look forward to every night.

SAULINA. Most of the artists I know can't afford to live in New York anymore. Too many of Jeffrey's friends buy their supposedly filmmaker children from Brown lofts. There's no space left in the city for practicing artists anymore.

JEFFREY. Is that why you canceled your last show?

SAULINA. Excuse me?

JEFFREY. I'm just trying to follow your logic. I thought maybe you canceled your last show because all my friends' filmmaker children took over your space.

SAULINA. I canceled because I wasn't ready.

FLINTY. That's the thing about my work. You can never really cancel a benefit. You always have to meet your deadlines.

SAULINA. I'm afraid I haven't been able to do that, Flinty, since my sister died. It didn't seem to affect Jeffrey's work at all, but I haven't touched mine since.

JEFFREY. Saulina, why don't I have Henry get you a car so you can go home? Ovid probably should have mentioned inviting you.

SAULINA. Don't blame Ovid for my coming. It was my choice.

JEFFREY. I don't blame him. I'm delighted to see you. Flinty here is thrilled to meet you. You're the one who seems to be on edge.

SAULINA. Stop it, Jeffrey.

JEFFREY. Stop what?

SAULINA. I don't have the energy to deal with you.

JEFFREY. Like I said, anytime you're ready, Henry will get you a car.

SAULINA. I'm just going to stand here and smoke.

JEFFREY. I'd prefer that you didn't.

SAULINA. Why? Have you heard cancer runs in my family?

JEFFREY. If you must, I prefer that you smoke in the garden.

Flinty, would you like to see the library?

(SAULINA opens the doors to the garden. She lights a cigarette. FLINTY and JEFFREY exit. OVID runs into the room.)

OVID. Aunt Saul, how weird was it when you guys walked in on us.

SAULINA. *(Immediately pulls herself together and puts out her cigarette.)* It wasn't weird at all. I'm sure Mr. Pfeiffer only wishes he had the same opportunity when he lived in your room. Is Caroline a friend from school?

OVID. No, I just met her tonight.

SAULINA. Ovey, that's fast work.

OVID. My dad meets people all the time.

SAULINA. I don't think you should base your romantic life on your father. Your father is a master at playing the world to his advantage.

OVID. He's not that bad.

SAULINA. Oh, come on, Ovid, what kind of world has he gotten you mixed up in? Do most of your friends live like this?

OVID. Sure. One of my friends' dad is buying the Museum of Natural History, but they're having a hard time finding a housekeeper.

SAULINA. When your dad and I were in college, this house would have been the last place he'd imagine himself living in. It was his idea for us to teach together in that Head Start program. In those days your dad would have ripped this party to shreds.

OVID. He would never have been invited. And my dad would hate that. This way he controls it. He can go in and out.

SAULINA. He told you that?

OVID. No. I figured it out. I spend a lot of time figuring him out. I'm going to write about my dad sometime, like Dreiser or Trollope, except shorter.

SAULINA. Just don't teach yourself to be as ingratiatingly logical as he is. It's not necessary to win every argument.

OVID. My mother used to say that.

SAULINA. I was her sister.

OVID. It's so strange she's not here. I mean not at this party. Just here.

SAULINA. I know. On my ride uptown tonight I looked for the lights in your mother's and then my parents' apartment windows. First 63rd and Park, the far right corner, second floor, then 75th and Madison, the double-height ceiling. I used to always silently wave hi or whisper goodnight. Funny, I have no idea who really lives up here anymore.

OVID. My dad and I are still here for you, Aunt Saul.

SAULINA. Poor Ovid. I wish I could release you from pleasing all of us.

(Enter VIVIAN, SID, CAROLINE, and PENNY.)

PENNY. Sid, there's no closet space in this house.

SID. So you buy the house next door and break through. Saulina, did Shirley show you his old playroom? Now that's what I call a fucking playroom!

SAULINA. Who's Shirley?

VIVIAN. I believe that's me.

SAULINA. His name is Vivian.

PENNY. Sid, there's nothing wrong with your playroom.

OVID. You have a playroom?

SID. It's really my screening room.

PENNY. He keeps all his toys in there.

SID. You'd really like it, Saulina. I've got a couple of Rauschenbergs hanging in there and a Schnabel on the way.

CAROLINE. He orders them to go.

SID. My favorite fucking people in the world are artists. Caroline, why don't you go see if that friend of your father who edits the *Times* is still in the garden. It wouldn't hurt if you'd go over and say hello. Am I right, Ovid?

CAROLINE. You are such a hypocrite! You show up at a formal dinner in a T-shirt and jacket just to show how hip and above it all you are, but the truth is, you take it all much more seriously than anybody else.

PENNY. I think you're being unfair. Your father is creative, and his attire is completely appropriate.

CAROLINE. Well, I don't have as much at stake in this as you do.

SID. Apologize to my wife. Now.

CAROLINE. Why? You mean you're not her ticket to Breast Express and the panty business?

SID. Penny happens to be the most successful online lingerie designer in the world.

CAROLINE. I know. That's why she was working at the Calvin Klein counter at Saks when you met her. She was apprenticing.

SID. Get the hell out!

OVID. I'll take you home, Caroline.

(FLINTY and JEFFREY reenter.)

FLINTY. I just met Alan Greenspan. He's adorable.

JEFFREY. Sean tells me that the buffet is served. Ovid, Sean said he made you vitello tannato.

OVID. Dad, I'm taking Caroline home.

SAULINA. Hell, I'll take you both out for dinner.

JEFFREY. Ovid, you promised to escort each of our guests on a private tour of the house.

OVID. Dad, if they're big enough to get invited to this party they can certainly manage to escort themselves around this house.

SAULINA. Or they can send their personal assistants.

JEFFREY. Why are you determined to spoil this evening?

SAULINA. I'm not. I'm going to dinner with Ovid and his friend. Would you like to join us, Mr. Pfeiffer?

JEFFREY. Ovid, your vitello tannato is getting cold.

OVID. It can't get cold, Dad, it's a cold dish.

JEFFREY. Ovid, I'd like you to stay.

OVID. Dad, I've decided. I want to take Caroline home.

SID. Ovid, I haven't had a chance to really talk to you yet.

CAROLINE. Why do you want to talk to him? Ovid can't get you on that museum board.

SID. I said get the hell out!

SAULINA. Let's go, Ovid. Mr. Pfeiffer?

JEFFREY. Ovid, it's the wrong choice.

SAULINA. And you know all the right ones.

JEFFREY. Not all. But in this case. Ovid, this really matters to me.

OVID. Dad ....

SAULINA. Ovid, now!

CAROLINE. I give up. Let's just stay here.

JEFFREY. Thank you, Caroline.

CAROLINE. You're welcome.

FLINTY. Ovid, you're so lucky to have such a firm father.

JEFFREY. Shall we go inside? It's getting late.

OVID. Don't worry, Dad, we're right on schedule. It's going great. Besides, at the turn of the century supper wasn't served until ten p.m. Am I right, Mr. Pfeiffer?

VIVIAN. Yes. And the meal of choice was lobster thermidor.

(OVID and CAROLINE exit.)

SID. The youth market is completely unpredictable. One minute they want sex and violence, and the next minute stability and Disney. Family's all that really matters. There's no one I'm more grateful to on this earth than my parents. Isn't that right, Penny?

PENNY. Yes, Sid. You are overwhelmingly attached to your mother.

SID. *(Kisses her.)* Jeffrey, you know what's so great about being a man? You've always got your life ahead of you. I thank God every day I was smart enough to start again with this wonderful woman. She is my perfect pitch, my polish, my guide. This woman has two degrees in decorative arts.

PENNY. I always tell Sid life can be wonderful. You just have to figure out a way to pay for it.

(SID and PENNY go in to dinner.)

SAULINA. Goodbye, Mr. Pfeiffer. Thank you for the tour. Good-night, Jeffrey. *(Exits.)*

JEFFREY. Well, let's go in to dinner. Mr. Pfeiffer, after you.

VIVIAN. Please go in to supper. I mean dinner. I'll be right there.

(JEFFREY exits. FLINTY notices as VIVIAN grabs on to a chair.)

FLINTY. Are you all right?

VIVIAN. I'm fine.

FLINTY. Can I get you something? Some water?

VIVIAN. No. I'll just sit and take in the room for a minute and listen to the music.

FLINTY. Do you mind if I join you for a sec?

VIVIAN. Not at all.

FLINTY. *(Sits down.)* I usually try to rest only when no one is watching. You know, Bernstein has a reputation for being a prickly guy. Brilliant but a social enigma.

VIVIAN. He's throwing this party. That's very sociable.

FLINTY. It's the middle of August! I wouldn't have advised it. But maybe that's why I'm just a party planner and he's Jeffrey Bernstein. You've got to be a little prickly to be at the head of the pack.

VIVIAN. Yes. Probably.

(FLINTY gets up.)

VIVIAN. Rest period's over?

FLINTY. It really isn't right to keep your host waiting. Let me know if I can get you anything?

VIVIAN. I'm fine. Thank you.

(FLINTY walks inside. VIVIAN moves his body slowly, as if one side is clearly in more pain. MARY GALLAGHER enters with drinks. She offers water to VIVIAN. PFEIFFER enters with BERTHA BREVOORT, the grand dame of New York society, played by the same actor who plays PENNY. She wears a gray wig and carries a fan.)

PFEIFFER. This way, Mrs. Brevoort.

BETINA. Tobias, it's almost ten o'clock. Where are your guests? It really isn't right to keep your host waiting.

PFEIFFER. It was so kind of you to interrupt your summer for our supper tonight.

BETINA. I take our museum very seriously, Tobias. I heard about Mr. Strauss's donation. We mustn't encourage newcomers to believe the world is open to them just because they can pay for it. Fortunes come and go, but it's quality and history that matter. Don't you agree?

VIVIAN. Mrs. Brevoort, your ancestors were Dutch pirates.

PFEIFFER. I couldn't agree with you more. If you'll pardon me. I'll go find Miss DeRoot.

BETINA. Yes. She's charming!

(BETINA takes out her fan. ARNOLD STRAUSS, played by the same actor who plays JEFFREY, comes into the room.)

ARNOLD. Mrs. Brevoort. I'm Arnold Strauss.

BETINA. It's a pleasure to meet you, Mr. Strauss.

VIVIAN. Mr. Strauss, I'm sure you know that Betina Brevoort was the grand dame of New York society circa 1917. She was celebrated for having a perfect sense of taste and propriety. Her great, granddaughter was recently arrested for dealing cocaine out of the Groton School basement.

BETINA. I'm sorry Mrs. Strauss isn't with you. Is your wife a Rothschild or a Montefiore or one of your other wonderful families?

ARNOLD. My wife is Mindy Rosenthal of Whitefish Bay, Wisconsin.

VIVIAN. Not to worry, Mr. Strauss. For the past thirty years I've been the Arnold and Mindy Strauss Professor of New York City History at Columbia University.

(A woman, SALLY WEBSTER, walks in wearing a turban hat and highly decorative jacket. She looks close to outrageous or haute bohemian. SALLY is played by the same actor who plays SAU-LINA.)

SALLY. Sorry I'm late. I blame it all on my yoga.

ARNOLD. I beg your pardon.

BETINA. Sally, I don't think you know Arnold Strauss from the Strauss Department Store. He's the candidate for the board of our little museum. He's already made a donation.

SALLY. Marvelous. Best thing to do is jump right in! I drove my automobile up here from the village.

STRAUSS. You drove your own automobile?

VIVIAN. Arnold, you might not know that Sally Webster was one of the great American diarists, long before Mabel Dodge ever had a diary.

SALLY. Don't you find the twentieth century thrilling, Mr. Strauss?

(PFEIFFER reenters the room with FLORENCE.)

FLORENCE. Please forgive me. Schuyler and I were just making plans for the garden. He'll be right in.

BETINA. That man should be in jail. And to think he designed both my club and my library.

SALLY. Maybe you should burn them both.

VIVIAN. I think I'm falling in love with you.

FLORENCE. Schuyler says I can help him with the garden gazebo.

VIVIAN. Schuyler Lynch, the architect of this house, always wore a white flower in his lapel.

(He takes a white flower from a vase, puts it in his lapel and stands up, transforming into SCHUYLER.)

SCHUYLER. The gazebo will give Mr. Frick next door something other than his paintings to look at.

STRAUSS. I hear Mr. Frick has lovely Vermeers.

PFEIFFER. Those paintings are too goddamned small! Give me Botticelli, Raphael anytime. Mr. Strauss, do you know what I do past midnight? I sit in front of my paintings, have a drink, and find my only peace.

TOBEY. *(Walks into the room.)* Good evening.

SALLY. Tobey, I thought you were up at school training this summer.

BETINA. None of the girls from our good families are in town, you know.

STRAUSS. My daughter Rachel is just back from Europe. Perhaps you should pay her a call. She's starting Radcliffe in the fall.

BETINA. How is it that you people all manage to be so intelligent?

TOBEY. Sorry, Mr. Strauss, I'm going to be in Europe next week, so I won't be able to. I've enlisted.

PFEIFFER. That's goddamned ridiculous!

SALLY. I think it's splendid Tobey! See the world! Get posted to Arabia! Climb the pyramids! Become a communist! Bravo! *(Does a grand curtsey to TOBEY.)*

PFEIFFER. Has anyone very told you that you're a goddamned spoiled and ridiculous woman?

BETINA. Tobias, please! If you argue, we'll never get to dinner and our vote on Mr. Strauss.

PFEIFFER. Please forgive me, Miss Webster. I'm just a coal miner's son from Uniondale. It's all blown over now. Everything's settled.

TOBEY. Nothing is settled, Father. I'm leaving next week.

FLORENCE. Mary, could you tell the musicians we'd like some supper music? Mr. Strauss, you're so intelligent, what music do you enjoy at supper.

ARNOLD. *(Laughing.)* A little Strauss.

FLORENCE. Oh, you are witty! Actually, they do a very nice contemporary suite. *(Takes him under the arm, and they go in to dinner.)*

PFEIFFER. Come along Miss Webster. I hear you're planning a trip to India. *(Takes SALLY under the arm.)*

BETINA. Mr. Lynch?

SCHUYLER. I'll be right with you.

PFEIFFER. That's right, Schuyler. Take a minute and talk some sense to Tobey. You both let your artistic sensibilities get the best of you. Mrs. Brevoort? I'm sure you're both looking forward to your lobster thermidor. *(Escorts SALLY and BETINA in to dinner.)*

TOBEY. Mr. Lynch, I can see the life my father has mapped out for me, and I want no part of it. I want to do work that means something to me.

SCHUYLER. You don't think your father's work means something to him?

TOBEY. My father's work gives him the right to have opinions about what other people do.

SCHUYLER. And you want to be able to look at something you've made and say, I took the time to polish that. I made the choice to put that color just off to the right. I invented that curve, and I looked it over nightly until I thought it was near perfect.

TOBEY. That's it! If I were you, every time I stepped inside the school chapel, I'd think. "Schuyler Lynch designed this!"

SCHUYLER. But you don't think Tobias Pfeiffer paid for it. It's called the Tobias Pfeiffer Chapel.

TOBEY. My father wants to see his name on your building, because somewhere he knows it's the one thing he can't do.

SCHUYLER. I worry for you, Tobias Vivian Pfeiffer II. You have the yearning of an artist. *(Kisses TOBEY's forehead.)* Against a tidal wave of obstacles, you had tonight the most brave and virtuous heart. *(Looks at him and pauses.)* Father, I do have a question I need to ask you.

TOBEY. Schuyler, it's me. Tobey. Are you all right? You look pale.

SCHUYLER. Father, I came because I need to know ....

TOBEY. Schuyler, sit down. Have a glass of water.

SCHUYLER. *(Regaining his composure.)* I'm terribly sorry. I'm fine. You should probably go in to dinner now. I mean supper. I just need to have a quick look at this door. It's been driving me mad all night.

TOBEY. That's my secret passageway! How do you know about that?

SCHUYLER. Young man, I know every inch of his house.

(TOBEY leaves the room. SCHUYLER tries to open the door, and SAULINA crawls through. As she does, SCHUYLER transforms into VIVIAN.)

VIVIAN. Saulina!
SAULINA. I came back for my sculpture. I'm never setting foot in

this house again, and I don't want Jeffrey to have it. I'll give it to you.

VIVIAN. I live in a one-bedroom on Claremont Avenue.

SAULINA. We'll store it at my studio. One day Jeffrey will tire of this house and start a newspaper, a bank or a preschool here. I won't have my work lost in his shuffle.

VIVIAN. You're much too cynical.

SAULINA. You're much too forgiving.

VIVIAN. I'm not. But I'm old. And I don't want to die a bitter man.

SAULINA. You don't seem bitter.

VIVIAN. But I am dying. Liver, pancreas, the whole kit and caboodle. That's why I accepted Ovid's invitation.

SAULINA. I'm sorry.

VIVIAN. No need. I just wanted to see the house I was born in. I've always admired structure. There's something to be said for solid beginnings, middles, and ends.

SAULINA. Oh, I'm a big fan of chaos. Maybe that's why my life has made no sense.

VIVIAN. Most lives make no sense. Some are just better orchestrated.

SAULINA. Maybe that's true. When my sister was alive, she'd invite me to escort her to these benefit dinners. For the women around these tables, life seemed to make utter and complete sense. In the mornings they lifted weights and at night they lifted their ten ton Harry Winston diamond brooches. I advised my daughter to strive to become one of them.

VIVIAN. You advised your daughter to become a woman with a brooch?

SAULINA. She didn't listen. My daughter is currently teaching English somewhere in the rainforest. My daughter has no area code, and she doesn't approve of e-mail either. She refuses to confront the twenty-first century.

VIVIAN. She's brave like you! Is she beautiful like you?

SAULINA. She's beautiful, yes. Looks more like her father.

VIVIAN. Do you see him?

SAULINA. No. Not since she was two. *(Pause.)* I like your flower.

VIVIAN. *(Takes another flower from the vase.)* I brought one for you too. *(Puts it in her lapel.)* We had dances in this room when I was a child. On Saturdays the boys and girls from the best New York families assembled here to display the box step and waltzes they mastered at Miss Kitty Frelinghuysen's Dancing School. The girls wore bronze slippers, and the boys miniature tails and black tie. I hid from all of them inside that doorway.

SAULINA. You must have broken a few hearts. Some girl must have been waiting patiently for you to ask her to dance.

VIVIAN. Will you?

SAULINA. Now?

VIVIAN. Just for the record, my health is currently in an upswing. I just passed my final exams with flying colors. Do you know the gavotte?

SAULINA. Sounds like a French and Yiddish cake.

VIVIAN. It was originally a peasant dance in quadruple meter introduced at the court of Louis XIV. Don't worry, I'll lead. *(They dance around the room. He dances quite gracefully. Suddenly VIVIAN stops dancing and looks at SAULINA.)* Saulina Webb, when I look back on my life I have very few regrets. But I always wanted to dance just once around this room. I think you are a truly gallant and generous woman.

SAULINA. Thank you. Really. Thank you so much. *(She starts to cry.)* I'm sorry. I'm so sorry.

VIVIAN. It's all right. Cry, Saulina. Cry for me. And cry for your sister Jessica. Cry of Ovid and Caroline too. Just cry for all of us.

SAULINA. I used to tell my daughter it was OK to cry because the tears would wash all the sad things away. And then everything would be all fresh and new.

VIVIAN. Until it all comes back again. And the true pattern of a life emerges.

SAULINA. Yes. Like a gavotte in quadruple time.

VIVIAN. We'd better go move your sculpture.

SAULINA. No, Vivian, we'd much better keep dancing.

(As they continue to dance, MARY GALLAGHER comes back into the room and begins clearing the glasses from the table. TOBEY

rushes into the room. VIVIAN and SAULINA continue to dance.)

TOBEY. Mary. I've been looking for you.

MARY. Just setting up for after supper, Mr. Pfeiffer. How was the party?

TOBEY. It's still going on. Mary Gallagher, would you do me the honor of one dance?

MARY. Mr. Pfeiffer, are you crazy? It's not my place. You should be at your father's table.

TOBEY. *(Lifts her up.)* No, Miss Gallagher, because from now on, I'll be making my own decisions for what I should be doing. I'm my own man now, Mary Gallagher. I heard this music and I thought, "Tobias Vivian Pfeiffer, II, all your life you wanted to dance with the prettiest girl in this house just once around this room."

(They dance. MARY curtsies to TOBEY.)

MARY. Thank you Mr. Pfeiffer. *(Begins to cry.)* You are very kind to me.

TOBEY. Don't cry, Mary. Everything is just beginning. Don't you know there'll be telephones that ring in Alaska, typewriters that write by themselves, and pajamas that never get dirty!

MARY. What?

TOBEY. Self-cleaning pajamas. It's my idea! Mary, people, not just social register people, will have decent houses with good schools and theaters in every town. Nothing will be the same! Not in painting, not in marriage, not in war! This will be the century of American ingenuity!

MARY. Sounds thrilling.

VIVIAN. *(To MARY;)* Yes. It was absolutely thrilling!

SAULINA *(To VIVIAN:)* I'm glad. So let's keep dancing.

TOBEY. *(To MARY:)* Do you mind if I ask if they'd change the music?

VIVIAN. *(To SAULINA:)* Do you mind if I ask if they'd change the music?

SAULINA. *(To VIVIAN:)* What would you like to hear?

TOBEY. *(To MARY:)* What would you like to hear?

VIVIAN and MARY. "After the Ball."
SAULINA. My sister loved that.
TOBEY. My mother loved that.

(TOBEY and VIVIAN begin singing.)

TOBEY and VIVIAN. *(Singing:)*
After the ball is over,
    ALL. *(Singing:)*
After the break of morn,
After the dancers' leaving
After the stars are gone;
    VIVIAN. *(Singing:)*
Many a heart is aching
If you could read them all;
    ALL. *(Singing:)*
Many the hopes that have vanished
After the ball ....

(They continue to dance as the lights fade.)

END OF ACT I

ACT II

(CAROLINE is singing "And the Band Played On." OVID plays the violin. JEFFREY and FLINTY, SID and PENNY, SAULINA and VIVIAN dance onto the stage as she sings.)

CAROLINE. *(Singing:)*
Casey would waltz with a strawberry blonde,
And the band played on.
He'd glide cross the floor with the girl he adored,
And the band played on.
But his brain was so loaded it nearly exploded,
The poor girl would shake with alarm,
He'd ne'er leave the girl with the strawberry curls
And the band played on.

(OVID grabs CAROLINE and they dance off with the others. FLINTY and JEFFREY dance back on from the other side.)

FLINTY. Christ, that band is never going to stop playing! *(Suddenly kisses JEFFREY quite passionately.)* Do you mind? I find sometimes it helps if I get the ball rolling.
JEFFREY. Have you ever considered investment banking?

(They kiss again. VIVIAN walks into the room. They don't notice him. VIVIAN leans against the table, and a book falls over. FLINTY turns around.)

VIVIAN. I beg your pardon. I thought I'd have a smoke in here. *(Lights a cigarette.)*

FLINTY. We were just inspecting the architectural details of the house.

JEFFREY. As I said before, I prefer you smoke in the garden.

VIVIAN. My grandfather had this room originally designed as a smoker. It has the most ornate details in the house. The room also held his favorite artworks. Botticelli's *The Last Communion of St. Jerome* right here. This was also the room in which my grandfather reversed the financial panic of 1907.

JEFFREY. Mr. Pfeiffer, I know you are a respected expert on New York City history, but it was J. P. Morgan who reversed that crisis in his own library.

VIVIAN. It was at my grandfather's initiation.

FLINTY. Do we really have to talk about his now?

VIVIAN. Forgive me for interrupting, Miss McGee. *(Exits into the garden.)*

FLINTY. Are you sure he was born in this house? Bernstein, I recognize class. He's sweet, but this is a man without a trust fund.

JEFFREY. His father left it all to good civic causes.

FLINTY. That's the sickest thing I've ever heard.

VIVIAN. *(Has overheard them.)* Excuse me, Miss McGee, but don't you believe in good civic causes?

FLINTY. Of course I do. No one has done more for the public library than me.

JEFFREY. Really? Not even Mrs. Astor?

FLINTY. Well of course Mrs. Astor! She's my idol.

JEFFREY. Flinty, they'll never knock the hunger out of you.

FLINTY. I know. I never rest.

(She kisses him and they fall down on the couch together. They are wildly making out. PFEIFFER walks in.)

PFEIFFER. Schuyler, why didn't you tell me it was this kind of party? You left me with Betina Brevoort babbling about the garden. Who is this man? I have the greatest admiration for him.

(VIVIAN puts a carnation in his lapel and transforms himself into SCHUYLER.)

SCHUYLER. This is the young man who bought your house.

FLINTY. *(Giggling.)* Bernstein, I'm falling.

PFEIFFER. Bernstein? My house was bought by a Jewish boy?

SCHUYLER. I believe so, but I wasn't precisely told.

FLINTY. *(Almost falls off the couch.)* Bernstein, let's go upstairs.

PFEIFFER. She's too thin. She's like making love to a Shaker chair. Schuyler, tell him to stay.

SCHUYLER. Mr. Bernstein, Mr. Pfeiffer wondered if you'd like to join him for a cigar and after-dinner drink.

JEFFREY. *(Sits up suddenly.)* Now?

SCHUYLER. It's after dinner. That's when they're usually served.

FLINTY. What's wrong, Bernstein?

JEFFREY. Is my friend invited too?

PFEIFFER. Schuyler, please inform my tenant that cigars and after-dinner drinks were traditionally male affairs.

JEFFREY. My friend happens to be a brilliant publicist plus one of the most desirable women in New York.

FLINTY. *(Gets up.)* OK Bernstein. Where's your room? We don't have much time. Sid and Penny will be wondering where we are.

PFEIFFER. Sid? Another Jew!

JEFFREY. It's a minyan.

PFEIFFER. What's that?

JEFFREY. When your particular crowd of males get together for cigars and after-dinner drinks. *(Turns to FLINTY.)* Flinty, I'm on the second floor.

PFEIFFER. *(To SCHUYLER:)* The entire second floor?

SCHUYLER. Gym, dressing room, bath, jacuzzi, media lounge, bedroom

PFEIFFER. All for him?

SCHUYLER. They're obsessed with staying in shape.

PFEIFFER. Thank God I just had to make money.

FLINTY. *(Kisses JEFFREY.)* I'll be in the jacuzzi. *(Exits.)*

SCHUYLER. Jeffrey Bernstein, this is Tobias Vivian Pfeiffer.

(They shake hands.)

PFEIFFER. Cigar? Or are you too damn healthy?

JEFFREY. No. Cigars have make an impressive comeback.

PFEIFFER. I am impressed.

JEFFREY. Gift of my friend Sid Nercessian. Hollywood producer.

PFEIFFER. I had producers, presidents, editors, curators, opera singers, generals and dictators smoking in this room. I even saved the country from a financial crisis here in 1907.

JEFFREY. Wasn't that J. P. Morgan?

PFEIFFER. Pierpont always had an eye for his own legacy. First meeting took place right here. It was I who first brought Morgan and the Jewish bankers together. I had Kuhn Loeb and J. P. to dinner. The next week Morgan locked us all up in his house and insisted we float the country a loan. Do you have that kind of power, Mr. Bernstein?

JEFFREY. Last month the president came here for a fundraising dinner. We charged $50,000 a plate. Sold out in a day.

PFEIFFER. Teddy Roosevelt called me personally before he started the Spanish-American War. I got Barings Bank of England to foot the bill for the whole goddamn thing. Do you have that kind of influence?

SCHUYLER. Mr. Bernstein is a master at high-risk arbitrage.

JEFFREY. For instance, it's possible I could make your entire fortune in just an hour.

PFEIFFER. Or you could lose it too. And furthermore it doesn't add up to a load of beans. Except money. In my day we were building a nation with steel, coal, and even though I hate to say it, Standard Oil. We were laying down railroads, inventing automobiles. You just move numbers. Tell me, Mr. Bernstein, what is your legacy?

JEFFREY. For one, I never abused the working man or attempted to bust a union.

PFEIFFER. Well, at least not directly.

JEFFREY. I know your stand on the steelworkers' strike. You lived in his house while those men were dying in shanty towns.

PFEIFFER. My son built concert halls and forty public libraries to make up for all that. Have you? I'll tell you what I think. You want no one else to have had a better time here than you.

JEFFREY. That sounds too much like entitlement.

PFEIFFER. Are you a left-wing hypocrite, Mr. Bernstein?

JEFFREY. No. But I was once a legal-aid lawyer. And I taught civics in a Head Start program.

PFEIFFER. So the purpose of your fortune is to make a better world?

JEFFREY. The purpose of my fortune is there's no glory in not having it. I want to be in the game because it's a very dull and inequitable world when you're not. You're forced to trust the system and at the mercy of mediocre bureaucrats. But if I'm rich, people want to know my opinion about newspapers, movie studios, and the Democratic Party.

PFEIFFER. Have more children, Mr. Bernstein. Children are who you leave behind. If I had to do it again I'd start a dynasty. I had three daughters who married barons and earls, but only one son. That was my one mistake.

SCHUYLER. Tobey wasn't a mistake.

PFEIFFER. He has a flighty imagination.

JEFFREY. Sounds like my son Ovid.

SCHUYLER. This is his photo, isn't it? He looks quite kind.

JEFFREY. That's not enough to survive in this world, Mr. Lynch.

PFEIFFER. In any world, Mr. Lynch.

JEFFREY. I'm afraid my jacuzzi is waiting.

PFEIFFER. She's a little too thin for my taste, Mr. Bernstein.

JEFFREY. You can never be too rich or too thin, Mr. Pfeiffer.

PFEIFFER. Bravo! That's just the sort of thing we could never say out loud in my day.

JEFFREY. I wasn't the first. *(Shakes his hand.)* It's an honor meeting you sir. Pleasure meeting you, Mr. Lynch. We tried hard to respect all your eccentricities.

PFEIFFER. *(Calls to JEFFREY as he leaves.)* Mr. Bernstein, how much does it cost you to keep that banister polished?

JEFFREY. About three hundred bucks a week.

PFEIFFER. *(Laughs.)* Oh that's good! That's very good!

(JEFFREY exits.)

PFEIFFER. Poor bastard. It's all about his money. Mr. Bernstein is cultivating a style, not a character. I should have been given more time. I need a drink. Sit down, Schuyler. Let me make you a whiskey and have a look at my painting. *(Begins to make a drink with his back to SCHUYLER.)* Doesn't it make you calm the way that the strong realist tendencies of the early Renaissance give way to an interest in emotion and poetry?

SCHUYLER. Tobias, you sound like a textbook.

PFEIFFER. You taught me that. *(Turns around.)* Where the hell is it?

SCHUYLER. What?

PFEIFFER. My painting. *The Last Communion of St. Jerome.* Where the hell is it?

SCHUYLER. Last I knew, it was in the Strauss Collection at the Metropolitan Museum.

PFEIFFER. Strauss, as in the peddler at my dinning room table tonight?

SCHUYLER. Your son sold it to him, and subsequently Strauss donated it to the museum. For some reason Strauss was obsessed with that particular work and paid a fortune for it.

PFEIFFER. You let this happen!

SCHUYLER. I designed his wing at the museum.

PFEIFFER. Why didn't you design my wing?

SCHUYLER. Let's just say I fell out of fashion.

PFEIFFER. Because of the scandal about you and that schoolboy at St. Paul's? I thought you just bought him a drink.

SCHUYLER. I did. I spent the remainder of my career designing community halls and gift shops in small towns in Vermont and Maine. Only Mr. Arnold Strauss went to bat for me.

PFEIFFER. I want my painting back.

SCHUYLER. I'm afraid it belongs to the people of the city of New York.

PFEIFFER. The hell with the people of the city of New York! The problem with you, Schuyler, is you were entirely too well-bred! But I won't be told by a Jew boy peddler, my ridiculous son, or a god-damn pansy with a flower in his jacket architect what happens to my painting! *(Takes the flower out of SCHUYLER's jacket and throws it on the floor.)* If I can save this country from financial ruin I certainly can reverse history! *(Exits.)*

(VIVIAN sits down slowly on the couch. He changes his position if in pain. He reaches to pour himself a glass of water. OVID and CAROLINE enter in costumes from the turn of the century.)

VIVIAN. *(Spills his water.)* Father, you should have never sold that painting!

OVID. What painting?

CAROLINE. Mr. Pfeiffer, are you all right? We were looking for you.

VIVIAN. Mary, may I have some water?

CAROLINE. Who's Mary?

VIVIAN. That's her dress you're wearing.

OVID. Mr. Pfeiffer, Caroline and I are the after-dinner entertainment.

CAROLINE. These are our costumes.

OVID. We found them in the attic.

VIVIAN. The entertainment. Of course. Yes, I see.

SAULINA. *(Bursts into the room.)* I have got to have a cigarette.

OVID. Aunt Saul, I thought you gave up smoking.

SAULINA. *(Lights up a cigarette.)* I did. You'll be glad to know that American's leading online designer of bikini thongs thinks Julian Schanbel is the greatest living artist and Cindy Sherman is much more important than Titian. Furthermore, her husband's favorite sculptor is Rene Ener. That's Rene spelled forwards and backwards, thank you very much, the twenty-four-year-old ex-addict who built a miniature golf course on her vagina. Jesus fuckin' Christ I need a drink.

OVID. Aunt Saul, I thought you stopped drinking.

SAULINA. *(Pours a drink.)* And now I've started again. Sometimes I ask myself why the hell I bother to keep sculpting. I should be taking pictures of myself playing Boggle on my breasts instead.

CAROLINE. What did he do to you?

SAULINA. Who?

CAROLINE. My father. We left you with him.

SAULINA. Your father. He didn't do anything. He just managed to erase my entire life's work.

CAROLINA. But my father is obsessed with artists.

SAULINA. Your father is obsessed with artists under thirty. The next wave, the cutting edge.

CAROLINE. You mean, like, anyone he can snort coke with.

SAULINA. The rest of us, according to Sid, are "fucking irrelevant."

CAROLINE. He said this in front of you?

SAULINA. Yes. But it's all right, because he has plans to make me important again. He can imagine Penny's lingerie launch at my next opening. My life and art could be a wonderland of Sid synergy. OK. End of tantrum. Ovid, let's get this show on the road.

VIVIAN. You're in Ovid's entertainment too?

OVID. My Aunt Saulina was always in all my shows, and my mother played the violin. Saulina even made her own costumes. She was a turkey for Thanksgiving and a potato latke for Chanukah.

SAULINA. Ovid, we can't do the play without our audience. Go find your dad before I come down with Toruette's syndrome again. *(OVID and CAROLINE exit.)* I was worried about you.

VIVIAN. I think I'm much more worried about you.

SAULINA. I'm such a hypocrite! All I wanted was for that horrid man to say "Saulina Victoria Webb, I include you in my list of all-American greats." And I hate myself for that much more than I could ever muster up hating him.

VIVIAN. Saulina, you can't look for profundity everywhere. You'll waste your life being bitter and alone.

SAULINA. I've already crossed that bridge and gotten to it. I can't bear to be judged anymore. I'm losing both the energy and the arrogance to pretend I don't care.

VIVIAN. You know, if my current schedule wasn't quite so erratic, I'd say to hell with them all. Let's have a long and torrid affair. *(SAULINA laughs.)* Why are you laughing?

SAULINA. It's been a very long time since I believed I was a girl.

VIVIAN. You're a girl, Saulina, and if my life were different, nothing would make me happier than to prove that to you. *(Takes her hand.)* Why won't you look at me?

SAULINA. Because I don't want to even think about losing you like I lost my sister. I'd much rather be numb.

VIVIAN. We're not doomed to be solo artists.

SAULINA. Then why are we?

VIVIAN. Maybe it took this long to find each other. Don't make the same mistake I did. Fall in love, Saulina. Don't waste your life alone.

(SID and PENNY enter.)

SID. Saulina, all this time Martha Stewart had you confused with Judy Chicago, but I told her who you were. Boy was she impressed!

VIVIAN. What's Martha Stewart doing in New York in August?

PENNY. Christmas catalogue time. I've been looking at fur-trimmed panties all day long.

SAULINA. Really!

PENNY. I saw them first in Lapland. Sid was shooting *Call of the Wild III* there.

VIVIAN. Sounds very uncomfortable.

SID. Shirley, it's for the boudoir.

SAULINA. His name is Vivian!

SID. Sorry fella, I knew it was one of those pretentious English girl ones. I've got a script out to Jeremy Irons to play a psycho killer Oxford don named Beverly. Cate Blanchette says she'll do the wife. Can she act or what? I get shivers down my pants. She blows me fuckin' away.

PENNY. Sid, I'm having a very hard time ignoring you tonight.

SID. Saulina, you know why my wife puts up with me? When you have perfect taste, you need to acquire a lifestyle to practice it.

PENNY. Why are you telling her this?

SID. You're both artists. She knows artists need to be supported.

PENNY. I'm not an artist. I'm a businesswoman. I just have my opinions. Saulina, what do you think of this house? Personally, I'd keep the bones and open the rest right up. You're an architectural historian, Mr. Pfeiffer. Why would anyone want to restore Schuyler Lynch? No one ever mentions him. I'd get Charlie Gwathmey in here and gut it.

(CAROLINE and OVID come back into the room with JEFFREY and FLINTY.)

CAROLINE. We found them!

FLINTY. We were upstairs inspecting the architectural details.

CAROLINE. She was just freshening up.

JEFFREY. *(Curt.)* Ovid, it's either time for your entertainment or I'm being rude and avoiding our other guests.

SID. Wait a minute! What about my board membership? You know, Geffen says I should just start my own museum and fuck it.

SAULINA. Sid, just for the record, my sister Jessica was on the board of the Metropolitan. That's how Jeffrey first got involved.

JEFFREY. Saulina, everyone knows you and your sister were from a distinguished new York family.

SAULINA. I just want my friend Sid here to know the reason you're in the position to bring his name up is because of her.

JEFFREY. Everyone on the board is still very grateful for Jessica's contribution.

SAULINA. You see, Sid, Jeffrey's interest in art is very recent.

JEFFREY. Sid, I'll bring your name up at the next nominating committee. Should be no problem.

SAULINA. By the way, Sid, you have my vote! Hell, I say put the entire hall of armor in Bite Me polka-dot briefs.

SID. Saulina, you're such a passionate woman! It must be where your art comes from.

CAROLINE. Sid, you're so full of shit!

JEFFREY. OK, Ovid. That's it. Time for your show. Mr. Pfeiffer, lead the way. Saulina, Penny, Sid.

SID. Please go on. We'll be right there. *(Takes CAROLINE's arm.)*

CAROLINE. But Daddy, I'm in the play.

SID. We'll be right there. *(When they have all left, he slaps CAROLINE.)* Don't ever talk that way to me in front of people again.

CAROLINE. Why? What will you do? Lock me up in an institution? My daughter's insane, doctor. I got on the museum board, but she knows I'm a complete fake. What will you do when *Entertainment Tonight* finds out?

SID. I won six Oscars last year and ten Golden Globe Awards. Nobody in the whole goddamned world thinks I'm a fake.

CAROLINE. That's because they're all fakes too.

SID. You think Harold fucking Pinter is a fake?

CAROLINE. You produced his movie. He doesn't care what kind of man you are.

SID. That's not true. Harold Pinter has real values. He's a fuckin' communist. I don't get you. You have everything going for you. You're smart, you're reasonably good-looking, you're unbelievably well-connected. Any one else would kill to be you.

CAROLINE. Why don't you hold auditions?

SID. What did I ever do to you? I divorced your mother. Not you. And I could have married a nineteen-year-old bimbo but I didn't. I married an accomplished, sophisticated woman. And you know why? I did that for you.

CAROLINE. Why did you ignore Saulina Webb?

SID. What the hell are you talking about?

CAROLINE. You were speaking about great artists in front of her, and you never mentioned her name.

SID. That's simple. She's not that good. She was interesting maybe fifteen years ago. Now, she's a bitter, angry, mediocre cow. That's just the truth.

CAROLINE. You have no heart.

SID. Sweetie, nobody has a bigger heart than me. Nobody in my business is more loved than me. Someday you'll realize that I know the pain you're in. I want to help you. I need a hug.

CAROLINE. What?

SID. I need a hug. *(Hugs her.)* I'm glad we cleared the air. Because you know nothing's more important to me than family. I stood up the entire Cannes film festival last year just to get back to your school play.

CAROLINE. You were casting your high school version of *All the King's Men.*

SID. You're so smart. *(Puts his arm around her.)* Are you still daddy's girl?

CAROLINE. Yes.

SID. I like this costume. Very upstairs parlor maid. If I wasn't your father ....

CAROLINE. But you are my father. Would you tell Ovid I'll be right there?

SID. I can wait.

CAROLINE. No, Daddy. It's a surprise. It's part of the show.

(SID leaves. CAROLINE breaks glass on the table and begins to slash her wrists. SAULINA walks in.)

SAULINA. Caroline! What are you doing? Caroline, give me that!

CAROLINE. I won't let him win.

SAULINA. And what about you?

CAROLINE. I don't care about me.

SAULINA. Well, I do. Let me see your hands.

CAROLINE. I haven't even made a dent. I usually get a lot further than this.

SAULINA. Really?

CAROLINE. It's unbearable, Saulina. Maybe he's right. Anyone else would be thrilled to be me. Maybe it's all my fault. But I just can't do it anymore.

SAULINA. I have very little wisdom, Caroline. But one thing I can promise you. If you and I try very hard, then they don't have to win. But if you give up, you'll never know how strong you could be.

VIVIAN. *(Walks into the room.)* Saulina, Ovid sent you to get Caroline and then you both disappeared. What's happened to your hand? *(Sits down.)*

SAULINA. She has a splinter.

VIVIAN. On both wrists?

SAULINA. It was twin splinters.

VIVIAN. Well, shall we go back in? We can't start the show without you. *(Begins to get up and can't.)* On second thought maybe you both go ahead.

CAROLINE. Mr. Pfeiffer, can I stay here with you. Ovid can sing with Aunt Saulina.

SAULINA. That's a very good idea. You rest here and Ovid and I'll get the show started. *(Exits.)*

(CAROLINE moves toward him. He flinches in pain from her touch.)

VIVIAN. Dear girl, just move your head a little bit this way. *(She puts her head on his shoulder.)* Yes, that's much better.

(Music begins to come in from the other room. It is a slow version of "Rag Time Doll.")

CAROLINE. Do you know this song? Ovid found it in a chest upstairs.
VIVIAN. Fifth-floor attic.
CAROLINE. That's the one. *(Begins to sing sweetly:)*
Hello ma baby
Hello ma honey
Hello my ragtime gal.
VIVIAN. You have a lovely voice.
CAROLINE. I'm going to be a singer. I'm changing my name to Cara C. Jones.
VIVIAN. *(Holds her.)* You'll be a wonderful singer, Cara C. Jones.

(As the music continues, TOBEY comes in playing an up-tempo version on the ukulele. He is followed by PFEIFFER, MR. STRAUSS, BETINA BREVOORT and FLORENCE DeROOT. They are clapping along with the song behind him.)

ALL.
Hello ma baby
Hello ma honey
Hello my ragtime gal.
Send me a kiss by wire
Baby, my heart's on fire!
TOBEY. *(Suddenly stops playing.)* Mary Gallagher, what's wrong with you?
CAROLINE. Who the heck is Mary Gallagher?
VIVIAN. She has a splinter.
TOBEY. Let me see. There should be iodine in the butler's pantry.
PFEIFFER. You're not even going to finish your song? Damn it

boy! Can't you do anything right?

    FLORENCE. Mary Gallagher, this is all your fault!

    TOBEY. Here, Schuyler. You take over.

    CAROLINE. Ovid, where are we going?

(TOBEY hands the ukulele over to VIVIAN and leads CAROLINE out of the room. SCHUYLER/VIVIAN finishes out the verse.)

    SCHUYLER.
If your refuse me
Honey you'll lose me.
    ALL.
Then you'll be left alone
Oh baby telephone
And tell me I'm your own.

(SALLY WEBB enters with a lobster headdress and claws. She sings the chorus.)

    SALLY.
Hello ma baby
Hello ma honey
Hello my ragtime gal.
Send me a kiss by wire
Baby, my heart's on fire!
    ALL.
If you refuse me
Honey you'll lose me
Then you'll be left alone
Oh baby telephone
And tell me I'm your own.

(SALLY and SCHUYLER dance together in a terrific rag. The audience applauds wildly.)

    PFEIFFER. *(Gets up.)* Bravo. Best performance by a crustacean I've seen in years.

SALLY. You like my claws? Louis Sherry helped me make them. I'm being served up at Delmonico's later tonight.

BETINA. *(To STRAUSS:)* Sally always likes to dress up as our main course.

FLORENCE. She once came as a baked Alaska and put herself on fire.

SALLY. My art is my life. I don't separate the two. Every minute is another opportunity to create.

SCHUYLER. Sally, would you marry me?

PFEIFFER. Fine idea. Have the wedding right here in the garden.

BETINA. Given your age, Sally, it's almost a miracle.

PFEIFFER. I went to the Kuhn Loeb wedding last week in the Warburg garden. They're creating a financial dynasty.

FLORENCE. You never told me you went to that wedding. Who did your bring?

SCHUYLER. Sally, I'm still waiting for an answer.

SALLY. Schuyler, I am forty-five years old. I have the most wonderful house on Bank Street, my family farm in Rhinebeck, and I tour Europe at least once a year. I think you are a gentle and fascinating fellow, but I have to say right now I'd prefer to keep my life just the way it is.

BETINA. Sally Webster, your life isn't remotely normal.

SCHUYLER/VIVIAN. I beg your pardon. I'm suddenly not quite feeling right.

PFEIFFER. Now let's vote on Mr. Strauss's board membership and finish the business at hand.

(TOBEY and CAROLINE walk back in.)

TOBEY. I couldn't get her splinter out.

SCHUYLER/VIVIAN. Tobey, is it very warm in here?

CAROLINE. Sid, what the hell is happening here?

FLORENCE. How dare you call Mr. Pfeiffer "Sid." Pack your bags, young lady. You're on the next boat back to Ireland.

CAROLINE. Ireland? I live on 79th and Park and go to Dalton. Ovid, are you all, like, on acid? Aunt Saulina, you've got a lobster on your head!

BETINA. Are you this child's aunt?

SALLY. Mrs. Brevoort, I am everybody's aunt. I am a Utopian Marxist Colony Club Libertarian.

CAROLINE. Mr. Bernstein please make them stop.

BETINA. *(Appalled.)* Is that your real name? Bernstein?

STRAUSS. I have no idea who "Bernstein" is.

CAROLINE. Ovid!

PFEIFFER. Young lady, there is no Ovid here. This is my son Tobias Vivian Pfeiffer II.

CAROLINE. Then this man is your grandson.

PFEIFFER. *(Yelling.)* Goddamn it, girl. That's Schuyler Lynch!

TOBEY. It's all right, father. Splinter's probably gotten infected.

PFEIFFER. Well, it's gone from her hand to her head.

SCHUYLER/VIVIAN. Yes. My head. Mary ....

CAROLINE. It's Caroline.

SCHUYLER/VIVIAN. Yes. That's right. Caroline. I'm sorry. I can't seem to keep you all apart anymore. It's all swirling together in my mind. Forgive me. I hoped I had more clarity. I shouldn't have brought you here. *(Takes CAROLINE's hand.)*

PFEIFFER. Please let's just goddamn vote on Mr. Strauss and then get a doctor for everybody here. *(Bangs a book on the table.)* This meeting of the nominating committee will come to order! All right, Mr. Strauss, I want you to look at that painting on the wall and tell me everything you see.

STRAUSS. The painting displays distinct Renaissance qualities. However, the realism gives way to an interest in emotion and poetry.

PFEIFFER. Did you coach him, Schuyler?

SCHUYLER. No.

STRAUSS. Although I'm sure this is the original, I would suggest that a number of copies do exist. I believe I've seen a pen drawing in my friend Mr. Lehman's collection.

BETINA. You people really stick together.

TOBEY. Father, this is intolerable!

PFEIFFER. Be quiet, Tobey. All right, Mr. Strauss. Who is the painter?

STRAUSS. I'd say Fra Filippo Lippi, around 1480.

PFEIFFER. Sorry. Botticelli, 1502.

SCHUYLER. Botticelli was actually a student of Filippo Lippi, so that's a pretty fair guess.

PFEIFFER. Really? If Strauss makes a guess like that for the museum we could end up passing on the *Mona Lisa*. I call the vote of the nominating committee to order. All those in favor. *(SCHUYLER and SALLY raise their hands.)* All those opposed. *(BETINA and FLORENCE raise their hands.)* The chair has the final vote. The nomination is denied.

TOBEY. Father, this is entirely unfair!

PFEIFFER. Who said life was fair, Tobias?

STRAUSS. *(Stands up.)* I'm afraid I must be getting home.

TOBEY. *(Shaking STRAUSS's hand.)* Thank you for coming to our house, Mr. Strauss. Next time I'm in New York, I would very much like to meet your daughter Rachel.

STRAUSS. Can you tell me the name of this painting again so I never forget it.

TOBEY. *The Last Communion of St. Jerome* by Sandro Botticelli. *(Takes STRAUSS's hand.)*

SALLY. Mr. Strauss, if you don't mind traveling with a crustacean, I could drive you home.

STRAUSS. Mr. Lynch, why don't you walk us to the car? Some air might do you good.

CAROLINE. He can't move.

SCHUYLER. I'm absolutely fine. Mr. Strauss, could you take this girl to see a surgeon at Bellevue for her splinter. It mustn't be misdiagnosed.

CAROLINE. I'm not going to Bellevue. Look, I'm fine. Not even a scar. You're no different from my fucking father.

PFEIFFER. Young lady, you're never to set foot in this house again!

TOBEY. Father!

PFEIFFER. I said be quiet, Tobey.

SALLY. By the way, Tobias, I'm taking my sculpture back.

STRAUSS. Miss Webster, I'll help you.

(They lift SAULINA's sculpture.)

PFEIFFER. Good. I never liked it.

BETINA. Tobias, please! This is getting out of hand.

PFEIFFER. It's ugly.

BETINA. I'm leaving. I have to get back to Newport.

PFEIFFER. Fine with me.

BETINA. Tobey, if you do go to war, be careful what you eat. And if you get lonely, I know some rather nice German families. *(Exits.)*

PFEIFFER. I don't know why you sent that sculpture to begin with.

SALLY. I hoped to open your eyes to the twentieth century.

(SAULINA, STRAUSS and CAROLINE exit with SAULINA's sculpture. SCHUYLER/VIVIAN remains on the couch. He is clearly in pain and intermittently dozes.)

FLORENCE. Tobias, who did you take to that Kuhn Loeb wedding?

PFEIFFER. Bloody hell, woman, I don't remember.

FLORENCE. Of course you remember! Was it that actress? The one with the red hair and the blousy arms who's always warbling "On the Banks of the Wabash" off-key. How could you? She so recherché. She actually eats at Luchow's.

PFEIFFER. Tobey, how 'bout an after-dinner drink?

FLORENCE. Oh, I know. It's Helena Rhinelander. Nothing would make you happier than to lock yourself into the Four Hundred. *(PFEIFFER is silent.)* I'm right. It was Helena Rhinelander! Tobias, she's probably seventeen.

PFEIFFER. Seems like a mature young woman.

FLORENCE. Are you going to marry her?

PFEIFFER. I know I'd like to have more children.

FLORENCE. She would never have wanted you if I hadn't taught you how to dress, how to eat. I was your polish. Your guide.

PFEIFFER. A decent butler could have done the same.

FLORENCE. Let me tell you something. One day, Tobias Vivian Pfeiffer, I'm going to have more money than you or any of your children. Because money means I won't have to base my life on a man whom I have no remote interest in. *(Walks out.)*

TOBEY. Father, are you really going to marry Helena Rhinelander?

PFEIFFER. I've never met her.

TOBEY. But ....

PFEIFFER. When you go into business, Tobey, you'll realize a time comes in every deal when you push your opponent to the edge and, inevitably, if they're even slightly shaky, they'll drop like flies.

TOBIAS. But I'm not going into business, Father.

PFEIFFER. You mean because of this nonsense about the war? *(Takes a letter from his pocket.)* I got a wire here from President Wilson. You're disqualified. You're too young.

TOBEY. No, I'm not. I'll be eighteen in September.

PFEIFFER. You're returning to St. Paul's School. Presidential orders. And you know what that cost me? I agreed to testify in Congress at an antitrust hearing. Idiots! Best thing that ever happened to this country were trusts!

TOBEY. You had no right to do that to me.

(VIVIAN wakes up.)

PFEIFFER. Feeling better, Schuyler? Schuyler?

VIVIAN/SCHUYLER. You'll be glad to know that Tobey here has decided to go back to school.

TOBEY. No, I'm not. I'm going to California to write shows.

PFEIFFER. And I'm going to Florence to paint like Botticelli.

TOBEY. I don't want to pay people to do what I dream about.

PFEIFFER. That's a stupid answer. I though at the very least you weren't a stupid man. Most important lesson I can teach you is always maintain control.

TOBEY. That's exactly what I'm trying to do.

PFEIFFER. Why? Because you think you're great?

TOBEY. What?

PFEIFFER. Do you think you're Bach, Beethoven, or Brahms?

TOBEY. Of course not. And that's not what I want to do.

PFEIFFER. Fine. Do you think you are John Philip Sousa? Can you tell me right now for certain your music will be as popular as "On the Sidewalks of New York?"

TOBEY. No. I'm not certain.

PFEIFFER. Then you're wasting your time. You're neither arrogant enough not to take orders nor talented enough not to give a damn what anybody says. You'll always be a pawn and second-rate. And I haven't built a fortune to have it whittled away by a second-rater. In a gilded age, Tobey, it's only a foolish man who doesn't take advantage. So what do you have to say?

TOBEY. Nothing.

PFEIFFER. You're weak, Tobey. A man with an independent vision would have walked out of this house and been on his way five minutes ago. *(Kisses TOBEY's forehead.)* You're a good boy. You're making the right choice. *(TOBEY doesn't reply.)* Cheer up Tobey. You'll have a great time after I drop dead and you start giving this family's money away. You can make our name synonymous with art and culture. Hell, build the Tobias Pfeiffer Opera house, and they'll play whatever ditty you write. They'll hire Puccini to write you an entire opera. Artists are cheap, Tobey. All they need is a little recognition. *(Kisses TOBEY's forehead.)* Schuyler, you missed the point of the whole shebang. Children. I'm planning to have at least six more in the second half of my life. *(Exits.)*

VIVIAN. Why didn't you just walk out?

TOBEY. Because he was right. Turns out he taught me a great lesson in life. The truth was, as an independent man I was fairly mediocre. As the keeper of a legacy I was far superior.

VIVIAN. Father, what gave you joy?

TOBEY. The day I sold Arnold Strauss my father's Botticelli. And you?

VIVIAN. I fell in love tonight with an artist named Saulina Webb.

TOBEY. Pretty girl?

VIVIAN. She has all the glorious finesse of a lobster thermidor.

TOBEY. There was a girl named Mary Gallagher, Irish girl, who worked in this house. I came home one August night from St. Paul's when there was an unexpected sweetness in the air and fell in love with her that night. Months later I heard from my father's cook that she had died of a splinter. Life is absolutely ridiculous.

VIVIAN. I'm fading, Father. I have a recurrent dream that the rest of the world is dancing forward while I make my final exit through the secret passageway.

TOBEY. You were a lucky man, Tobias Pfeiffer III. I freed you of a legacy.

VIVIAN. You denied me a legacy.

TOBEY. If you had a nickel more, you might have become a charming dilettante. The sort of gentleman who spends his days appreciating good books and art.

VIVIAN. I spent my life tracing New York legacies because mine was denied me.

TOBEY. I was protecting you. I gave you a chance to find some independent energy.

VIVIAN. And I failed?

TOBEY. No. You just politely stepped aside to make room for someone who wanted it more. Like the man who lives here now. As always you were a gentleman.

VIVIAN. You let my grandfather destroy your life.

TOBEY. If that's how you see it, you should be grateful I never meddled in yours.

VIVIAN. I never really felt I knew you.

TOBEY. You're a scholar, Vivian. Haven't you read? I redefined philanthropy.

VIVIAN. You were astonishingly selfish.

TOBEY. Nonsense. I'll go down as one of the most generous men in history.

VIVIAN. You gave away what cost you the least.

TOBEY. I'm sorry you felt short changed. *(Gives him a coin from his pocket.)* Here you go.

VIVIAN. What's that?

TOBEY. Old money. It's all yours. *(Exits.)*

JEFFREY *(Walks into the room.)* Mr. Pfeiffer, Sonny Mehta said he's sorry he didn't get a chance to say goodnight. I didn't know he was your publisher. Sonny said you wrote the definitive guide to the Upper East Side.

FLINTY. *(Enters.)* I just put Barry and Diane in their car. I absolutely adore Barry. I wish he would run for office. If only he could do for this country what he did for the Home Shopping Network.

JEFFREY. Where's Saulina's statue? Did she drag that thing out of here?

VIVIAN. She took Caroline to Bellevue.

JEFFREY. What? Does Sid know this?

(CAROLINE and SAULINA walk in.)

CAROLINE. Where's Ovid?

FLINTY. Are you all right?

SAULINA. She's fine.

CAROLINE. I had a splinter.

SAULINA. I gave my statue to Martha Stewart. Caroline helped me carry it.

JEFFREY. You went to Bellevue for a splinter?

SAULINA. Who said she went to Bellevue? Jeffrey, I'm a sculptor. I took care of her in my car.

VIVIAN. You are an astonishing woman!

PENNY. *(Walks in.)* Guess what? Charlie Rose just offered us a ride home.

(OVID comes back in a T-shirt and blue jeans.)

JEFFREY. What are you wearing? The party isn't over.

OVID. The guests are all leaving.

PENNY. Caroline, Sid said he'd leave his car for you.

CAROLINE. No thanks, I'm spending the night here.

OVID. You are?

CAROLINE. There's no where else I want to be.

OVID. Dad?

JEFFREY. You're a grown man, Ovid. It's up to you.

CAROLINE. Ovid, it's kinda like community service. You can get credit for it at Trinity.

OVID. Caroline, we would be delighted to have you as our guest tonight.

PENNY. Well, I better get home. Nighttime nanny goes off duty at 1 a.m. and I like to be there for the changing of the guard. *(Circles the room to say her good-byes.)* Flinty, we're having lunch Monday. I want to hear everything. So nice to meet you all. Jeffrey, I love this house. Don't change a thing. Caroline, I'll take care of Sid's car. And I'll take care of Sid.

CAROLINE. Thank you.

PENNY. You're welcome. Goodnight. *(Exits.)*

CAROLINE. Ovid, do you mind if I go upstairs. My splinters are aching me. *(Kisses him on the lips.)* Thank you for letting me stay. Goodnight. *(Exits.)*

FLINTY. Jeffrey, can I spend the night? There's no where else I'd want to be.

JEFFREY. I'm a little tired, Flinty. I have to get up early tomorrow.

FLINTY. I do too, I have to get back to the Hamptons by noon for lunch, and I've got a 2 p.m. baseball game.

JEFFREY. You have a full life. Thank you for fitting us in.

FLINTY. I can cancel them. I'd really rather spend some more time with you.

JEFFREY. I'm sorry, Flinty. I'm sure we'll run into each other at one of your events very soon.

FLINTY. Oh yes. Of course. Sure.

JEFFREY. Excuse me. I should say goodnight to our other guests. *(Exits.)*

VIVIAN. Are you all right, Ms. McGee?

FLINTY. Do you ever wonder what it's like to be them? It must be so wonderful when no one can ever say no to you.

VIVIAN. Maybe the trick is not to care.

FLINTY. Oh, I have to care. It's my entire life. I'm fine. Really. I'll order in some fries when I get home, think about redecorating my bedroom and get a good night's rest. I do that a lot on the weekends.

VIVIAN. Do you know that my grandfather's mistress, Miss Florence DeRoot, was a pioneer in décor. She invented the window treatment.

FLINTY. Really?

VIVIAN. Not to mention the modern dinner party.

FLINTY. Why on earth did your grandfather ever let her go?

VIVIAN. Her specific charms might have been much more appreciated today.

FLINTY. Don't you love the times we're living in? I see nothing but possibilities. I toast the twenty-first century.

VIVIAN. Yes. To the twenty-first century.

FLINTY. Goodnight, Mr. Pfeiffer. *(Kisses him on the cheek.)* I'll tell the *Chronicle* it was the party of the year. *(Exits.)*

SAULINA. Vivian, can I give you a ride home?

VIVIAN. If you don't mind, I'd like to take a final look at the garden.

OVID. Goodnight, Mr. Pfeiffer. Thanks for coming to our house.

(VIVIAN exits into the garden and OVID exits upstairs. JEFFREY re-enters the room.)

JEFFREY. Where's Ovid?

SAULINA. He went upstairs. Well, thank you for a lovely evening.

JEFFREY. Thank you for coming. Goodnight.

SAULINA. Jeffrey, if you prefer, I could walk out of here and never see you again.

JEFFREY. Do whatever you like. I've had enough women making threats tonight.

SAULINA. Goddamn it Jeffrey, you're so cold! I can't even find you.

JEFFREY. I'm right here.

SAULINA. No. You're hiding behind this party, this house, and these people!

JEFFREY. What's the matter with these people? Everyone in America wants to be with these people. I want to be with these people. You're out of touch, Saulina, and that's the problem with both you and your art. You're living in the past. Think about the future.

SAULINA. Do you ever tire of your entire life being so convenient? You've got it all worked out. Goodnight, Jeffrey. *(Begins to leave.)*

JEFFREY. Why did you bother to come tonight?

SAULINA. Ovid invited me.

JEFFREY. Not good enough.

SAULINA. I'm sorry I'm not up to your standards.

JEFFREY. Saulina, you've become impossible to talk to! The woman I met thirty years ago wasn't self-righteous and defensive.

SAULINA. Unfortunately, we all can't be restored to our former glory like this house.

JEFFREY. I remember when Jessica and I bought this house. She asked me, "Is this the way we're supposed to live now?"

SAULINA. *(Suddenly yelling:)* Who cares how you were supposed to live! I watched Jessica fade, and somehow you managed to vanish too. Where have you gone, Jeffrey?

(OVID reenters on top of the staircase.)

JEFFREY. Saulina ....

SAULINA. I miss my sister, Jeffrey, and I miss you.

JEFFREY. Saulina, I don't want you to never see us again. Ovid loves you.

SAULINA. Ovid and I will always be friends.

JEFFREY. Saulina, I promise you. The man in front of you is who I always wished I could be. If I wasn't who I am now, I'd waste my life envying this man's every waking breath.

OVID. Dad, are you happy?

JEFFREY. Ovid, who could live in this house and not be happy?

SAULINA. Me.

JEFFREY. I've come to the conclusion happiness is irrelevant. Money can buy you happiness.

OVID. Dad, do you really believe that?

JEFFREY. It takes care of most things very nicely.

VIVIAN. *(Returns from the garden.)* The musicians have packed up and gone.

SAULINA. Are you ready, Vivian?

VIVIAN. I think I need to rest a while.

SAULINA. It's funny, for the first time in months I have this odd desire to work tonight.

VIVIAN. *(Kisses her hand.)* Saulina. Anastamose!

SAULINA. I beg your pardon?

VIVIAN. A word I learned during one of my recent medical procedures. It's the process of two arteries becoming one.

SAULINA. Like Broadway and Fifth spilling into Madison Square?

VIVIAN. Precisely. Thereby creating the Flatiron Building. Erected in 1902 by Daniel H. Burnham. Standing twenty stories tall with a limestone-on-steel frame, the building became the city's first symbol for the modern skyscraper era. Goodnight, dear Saulina.

SAULINA. I will call you tomorrow.

VIVIAN. Yes. Please. Call me tomorrow.

SAULINA. Goodnight, Jeffrey. Flinty's right. It was the party of the year.

JEFFREY. It was Ovid's idea.

OVID. No it wasn't.

JEFFREY. He's a brilliant strategist.

SAULINA. Of course he is. He's his mother's son. *(Exits.)*

JEFFREY. Ovey check the secret passageway. Mr. Pfeiffer please stay as long as you like. Goodnight. *(Exits upstairs.)*

OVID. My father's life is stuck somewhere between Caesar Chavez and Baron Rothschild.

VIVIAN. You have the eye of a writer.

OVID. I spend a lot of time watching things. I have an idea for a novel.

VIVIAN. That's wonderful.

OVID. I can't do it unless I know I'm really good. I don't want to disappoint him.

VIVIAN. Ovid, you must do whatever it is for yourself. My father wanted to write music and never did.

OVID. Why?

VIVIAN. Maybe for the same reason I never really left this house. He was too scared.

OVID. But you became a writer.

VIVIAN. Yes, but I realize now I spent my entire life writing to get back here. I never escaped.

OVID. My father says that money is the road to liberation.

VIVIAN. Is your father really free?

OVID. What was the word you taught Saulina?

VIVIAN. "Anastamose!" When two separate streams flow into each other.

OVID. And converge?

VIVIAN. Or travel on a similar path.

OVID. Like my father and Miss McGee?

VIVIAN. Maybe. Or even like you and me.

OVID. I better check that passageway before some other girlfriend of my father's crawls in here.

VIVIAN. Is that what he's so worried about?

OVID. Oh, Mr. Pfeiffer, they come out of the woodwork.

VIVIAN. Well, better take care of that. I think I'll just make myself comfortable and enjoy Schuyler's ceiling.

(OVID exits. VIVIAN moves himself slowly on the couch. He lies down and pulls an afghan over himself. MARY GALLAGHER comes in.)

MARY. Mr. Lynch!

VIVIAN/SCHUYLER. Mary Gallagher. You're back!

MARY. They got my splinter out, Mr. Lynch. I'm fine.

VIVIAN/SCHUYLER. That's splendid news, Mary.

MARY. Are you feeling all right, Mr. Lynch?

VIVIAN/SCHUYLER. Yes. I'm thoroughly enjoying myself looking at the ceiling.

MARY. Can I see? *(Sits down on the floor beside him.)*

VIVIAN/SCHUYLER. Of course. Look, there's an elephant in the corner and a frog on his nose.

MARY. I never noticed that before. There's another one. how wonderful!

VIVIAN/SCHUYLER. Yes. Tonight this house is full of remarkable couplings.

MARY. I'm not going back to Ireland, Mr. Lynch. I'm staying right here. New York's my home.

VIVIAN/SCHUYLER. Isn't it a glorious city. East Side, West Side. All around the town.

MARY. I think Tobey wrote that song.

VIVIAN/SCHUYLER. Really? My father?

MARY. Well, at least he taught it to me.

VIVIAN/SCHUYLER. Mary Gallagher, would you do me the

honor of singing it once for me? I know I'll remember it for the rest of my life.

(MARY begins to sing softly.)

MARY.
Down in front of Casey's
Old brown wooden stoop,
On a summer's evening
We formed a merry group.

(FLORENCE, BETINA, STRAUSS, and PFEIFFER dance out and sing.)

ALL.
East Side, West Side
All around the town ….

(They all continue to hum the tune. VIVIAN sits down and closes his eyes. All except MARY and VIVIAN exit. OVID wears a corduroy jacket over his blue jeans and steps forward as MARY continues to hum "East Side, West Side" under his speech.)

OVID. When I dropped out of law school at Columbia, I rented a one-bedroom apartment on Claremont Avenue. The super told me about a Columbia professor who had lived there for fifty years. He had a rare collection of New York City maps. When he died, a truck arrived from the Pfeiffer Library to collect them. The super never imagined the unassuming gentleman could have a library named for him.

(VIVIAN looks as SAULINA walks on.)

MARY.
Pretty Nellie Shannon
With a dude as light as cork
First picked up the waltz step
On the sidewalks of New York.

(MARY continues humming the tune of "The Sidewalks of New York." VIVIAN gets up and dances with SAULINA. He kisses her deeply. He dances off with SAULINA. OVID continues his speech.)

OVID. My Aunt Saulina married again, one year before she died at fifty-three. Breast cancer runs in the chosen people's families. Her husband Anthony was a drawing teacher at Sheepshead Bay High. On the day she died, she whispered to me. "Fall in love, Ovid. Don't waste your life alone."

(JEFFREY, FLINTY, SID and PENNY dance out in their contemporary clothes.)

ALL.
Boys and girls together,
Me and Mamie O'Rorke ....

OVID. I wrote my first novel in that Claremont Avenue apartment which was very well received. I was even interviewed by Flinty McGee on her talk show. She married the chairman of a major international news organization, who she met while snowshoeing in Siberia.

Caroline never made it to Brown. She did however have a stint as Cara C. Jones, a country music singer. When Sid was arrested for snorting coke at his own premier, Caroline came to his rescue. She produced his version of *The Rivals,* which proved to be a summer blockbuster. Caroline is now president to Sony-Fox Nercessian pictures.

My father lived to be eighty-eight. He remarried a girl from the Rhinelander family. They had five more children, and in the late twenties my father became ambassador to Switzerland. I once asked him if he was happy, and he told me only losers have time to ask those questions. Even at eighty he'd take me aside and say, "You know, because of you I look at my new family and worry. It's hard to keep hunger in the next generation." "You'll get them, Dad, " I'd reassure him. "Yes," he'd answer, "But somehow I managed to lose you."

(OVID walks off. The actor playing VIVIAN returns in blue jeans and a jacket similar to OVID's. He now plays OVID as an older man.)

OLDER OVID. *(Singing:)*
Things have changed those times,
Some are up in "G,"
Others they are wand'rers,
But they all feel just like me.

ALL.
East Side, West Side,
All around the town,
Tots sang ring-a-rosie,
London Bridge is falling down.

(OLDER OVID watches as the centuries fold together. YOUNG OVID returns dancing with MARY, PFEIFFER and FLINTY, BETINA and JEFFREY. They all dance off. OLDER OVID is alone onstage.)

OLDER OVID. My novel about my father Jeffrey came in 2043. It was my sixtieth birthday present to myself. I have lived my entire life in New York City. I've written around twenty novels, some well received, some not. I married a music professor, and we live in Brooklyn near where my father grew up. He refused to ever visit us there.

My father's house is now a museum of the digital revolution with relics of the late twentieth century, like laptops, cellular phones, and paper money. My grandson insisted I bring him here before he went of to Sanford.

(OVID comes back onstage and plays his own grandson.)

OVID'S GRANDSON. You really grew up here?
OLDER OVID/VIVIAN. Yes. That banister cost three hundred dollars a week to clean.
OVID'S GRANDSON. That's all?

OLDER OVID/VIVIAN. Seemed like a lot then.

OVID'S GRANDSON. Did they still use paper money?

OLDER OVID/VIVIAN. For banisters and taxis.

OVID'S GRANDSON. Looks like a great place for parties.

OLDER OVID/VIVIAN. Oh yes. We had great parties. I remember one when I was your age. It was an August night. Everyone in New York was here.

OVID'S GRANDSON. One day I want a house like this. But I'm going to build it. I want the world to know I'm here.

OLDER OVID/VIVIAN. You would have liked my father, Jeffrey. He admired energy. He liked a grand gesture. I was the wrong fit for him.

OVID'S GRANDSON. Did he build this house?

OLDER OVID/VIVIAN. No. It was an industrialist around two hundred years ago. But I met his grandson, Vivian Pfeiffer. He spent his final night here.

OVID'S GRANDSON. You mean he died here?

OLDER OVID/VIVIAN. Yes. The night of the party.

OVID'S GRANDSON. That's sad.

OLDER OVID/VIVIAN. No. I think it was deliberate. He was a historian. He looked for patterns in life. But I never forgot him. He helped me decide to make my own way. I left this world, but now I'm lucky enough to come back here with you. C'mere, I'll show you the best part of the house. There's a secret passageway right here that led out to the street.

OVID'S GRANDSON. We can't go there!

OLDER OVID/VIVIAN. Of course we can.

OVID'S GRANDSON. It's a museum. What'll we do if they stop us?

OLDER OVID/VIVIAN. You want permission? *(Puts his hand in his pocket and takes out a quarter.)* Here. Some people used to think this would open any door. All problems solved.

OVID'S GRANDSON. What is it?

OLDER OVID/VIVIAN. It's yours. If anybody stops you, just show this to them and say "I am entitled to certain rights and privileges. This, my good man, is old money."

(He puts his arm around his grandson. They open the passageway and walk through together.)

END OF PLAY

Flight
ARTHUR GIRON

"A witty, touching flashback...There is poignancy between the laughs." —*The New York Times*

The author doesn't claim it happened exactly this way. He has taken real-life characters and biographical information and supposed what it was like for Orville and Wilbur growing up in the dysfunctional Wright family. They are portrayed as boys whose mischief is just a sign of frustrated brilliance. Not a documentary, the play explores the dynamics of the Wright family in theatrical terms. 4 m., 1 f. (#8179)

Pride's Crossing
TINA HOWE

Best American Play of 1998
New York Drama Critics Circle

"A play you will remember and forever cherish....It is rich in both texture and imagination."— *New York Post*
"A lovely achievement...Mabel becomes a woman who ... both typified her time and her class and transcended it."—*Variety*

At ninety, Mabel Tidings Bigelow insists on celebrating her daughter and granddaughter's annual visit with a croquet party. As the party unfolds, she relives vignettes from the past that reveal the precise moment of opportunity lost and love rejected that define her life. The vibrant portrait of Mabel that takes shape culminates in her one shining achievement when she became the first woman to swim the English Channel. 4 m., 3 f. (#18230)

Send for your copy of the Samuel French
BASIC CATALOGUE OF PLAYS AND MUSICALS

You Shouldn't Have Told
ANNE THOMPSON-SCRETCHING

Winner of the 1997 Jean Dalrymple Award
for Best New Playwright
"Cyclonic.... A sometimes hilarious, often searing
portrait of black urban America in the 1990s."
—*New York Post*

Standing-room-only audiences cheered the New York production of
this emotionally charged drama about a middle-class black family
coping with a shameful tragedy. This is the story of a decent mother
who refuses to believe her three daughters when they tell her that
her boyfriend is sexually molesting them until the youngest dies
from a botched abortion. It touches a nerve that crosses class and
cultural experiences. 4 m., 5 f. (#27610)

Mr. Bundy
JANE MARTIN

"Jane Martin has written her strongest play yet."
—*Theatrescope*

This powerful drama examines the fears of parents driven to do
"the right thing" to protect their daughter. Mom and dad learn that
their neighbor is a convicted child molester and consider both vigi-
lance and vigilantism before being forced into action by a pair of
child advocacy crusaders. The shocking climax hits a nerve, leaving
the audience to consider where the line between right and wrong
lies. This play was a hit at the 1998 Actors Theatre of Louisville
Humana Festival. 3m., 1f., 1 f. child. (#15295)

Send for your copy of the Samuel French
BASIC CATALOGUE OF PLAYS AND MUSICALS

The Judas Kiss
DAVID HARE

"What Hare has achieved masterfully are two companion vignettes pinpointing the fall of Wilde."—*New York Post*

"Shifts the heroic focus, emphasizing Wilde less as a martyr of sexual persuasion than a martyr of love."—*The New York Times*

"A moving evocation of the human spirit."—*New York Post*

Liam Neeson starred on Broadway in this compelling depiction of Oscar Wilde just before and after his imprisonment. Act I captures him in 1895 on the eve of his arrest; Act II portrays him in Naples two years later during a reunion with his unworthy lover. 6 m., 1 f. (#12645)

Never the Sinner
JOHN LOGAN

"Remarkable."—*The New York Times*

"Great theatre. One of the year's best! An excellent and compelling play!"—*The New York Post*

"Riveting."——*New York Daily News*

Why would stylish, wealthy and intelligent young men murder an innocent boy? What demons lurked behind Robert Leob's flashing good looks? Behind Nathan Leopold's saturnine intellect? This exquisite Off Broadway hit explores the complex, provocative relationship between these infamous killers in a love story set to themes of crime and punishment, the press, the times, humanism, Nietzsche's philosophy and the end of the jazz age. 7 m. (#16591)

Our *Basic Catalogue of Plays and Musicals* lists other plays by David Hare and John Logan.

Send for your copy of the Samuel French BASIC CATALOGUE OF PLAYS AND MUSICALS

Pilots of the Purple Twilight
STEVE KLUGER

Here is a comedy of manners set in the first class smoking lounge of the *Titanic* on the night she foundered. It highlights the nobility of those who chose, for varying reasons, to remain on board. Ida Straus could not let her beloved husband of so many years die alone. To John Jacob Astor, the richest man in the world, the self-sacrifice was a matter of etiquette. Discrimination played a part for Thomas Kilgannon, a laborer from County Galway who was locked in steerage until the lifeboats were away. While some liberties were taken to bring nine diverse personalities together on the night that most of them would perish, the individual stories are accurate and have long since become legends, if only to their families. 5 m., 4 f. (#18692)

The Sutherland
CHARLES SMITH

A promising musician comes of age during Chicago's 1950s south side jazz scene with Miles Davis, Duke Ellington and John Coltrane as his role models. Having embarked on a six-month European tour at the age of 18 and been seduced by their appreciation of jazz and a Viennese woman, he returns 15 years later. He had heard about the sixties race riots and now he sees the devastation they caused and the decline of the inner city neighborhood that was his home. He ponders his absence during those turbulent times as well as his current existence while sitting amongst the ghosts of the Sutherland Show Lounge, once a Mecca of jazz. Originally produced by Victory Gardens Theatre, *The Sutherland* won the Illinois Arts Council Governors' Award for Playwriting. 6 m., 2 f. (#21438)

**Our *Basic Catalogue of Plays and Musicals* lists
other plays by Steve Kluger and Charles Smith.**

**Send for your copy of the Samuel French
BASIC CATALOGUE OF PLAYS AND MUSICALS**

AUDIENCES LOVE THESE LIVE STAGE VERSIONS THAT INSPIRED POPULAR MOVIES

Hurlyburly

Glengarry Glen Ross

Crossing Delancey
and

A Few Good Men

Amadeus

Other People's Money

Agnes of God

Extremities

Brewster's Millions

Educating Rita

The Best Little Whore-
house in Texas

The Philadelphia Story

The Miracle Worker

Come Back to the Five
Dime, Jimmy Dean,
Jimmy Dean

Shadowlands

The Prisoner of Second
Avenue

The Odd Couple

Biloxi Blues

The Madness of George III

Death and the Maiden

Les Liaisons Dangereuses

These are among the thousands of plays in Samuel French's
BASIC CATALOG OF PLAYS AND MUSICALS

Samuel French, Inc.
THE HOUSE OF PLAYS SINCE 1830